ZWISCHEN DEN JAHREN

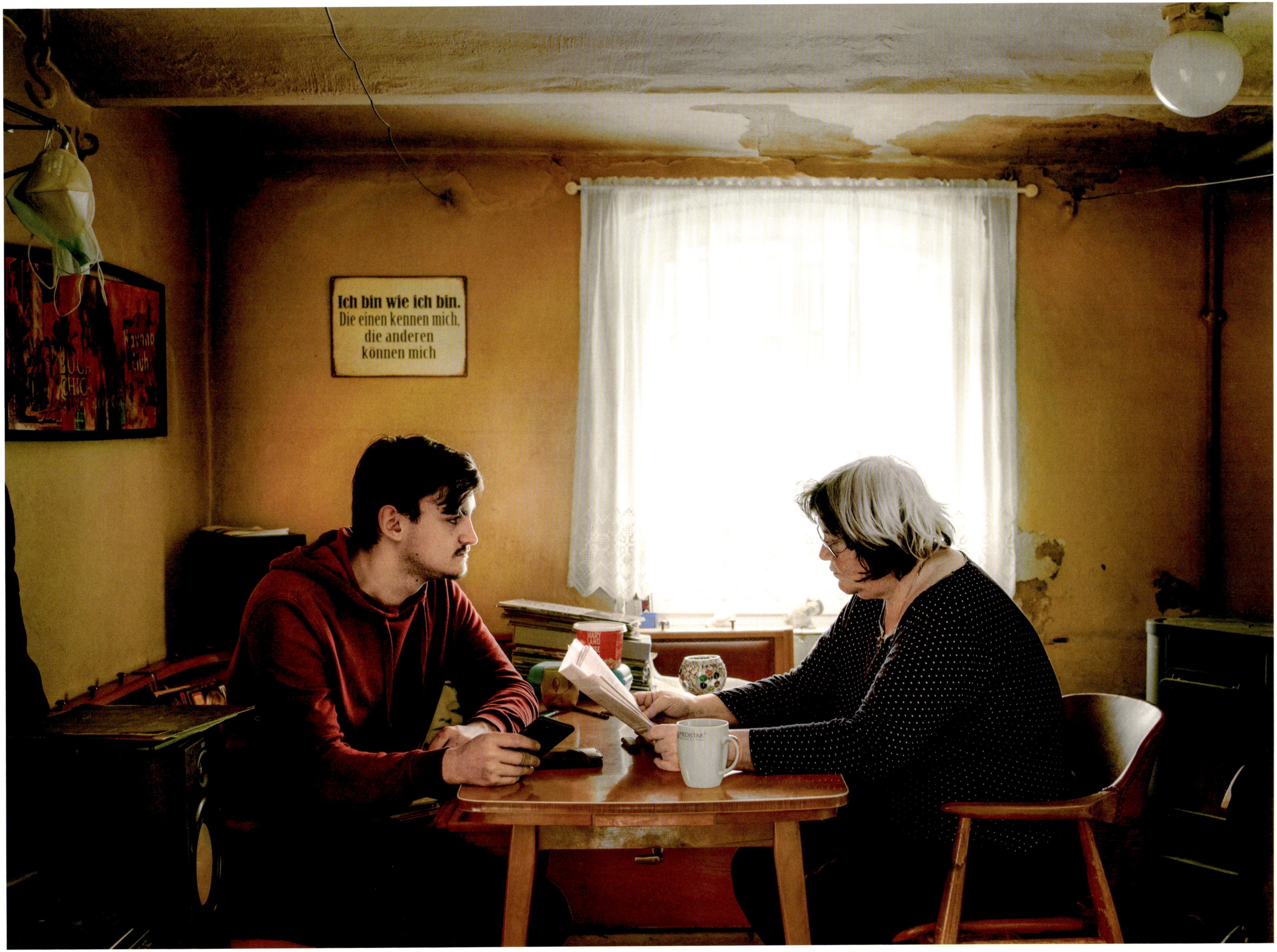
Ich bin wie ich bin.
Die einen kennen mich,
die anderen
können mich

V A L E N
T I N G
O P P E L

ZWISCH EN DEN JAHREN

GOST

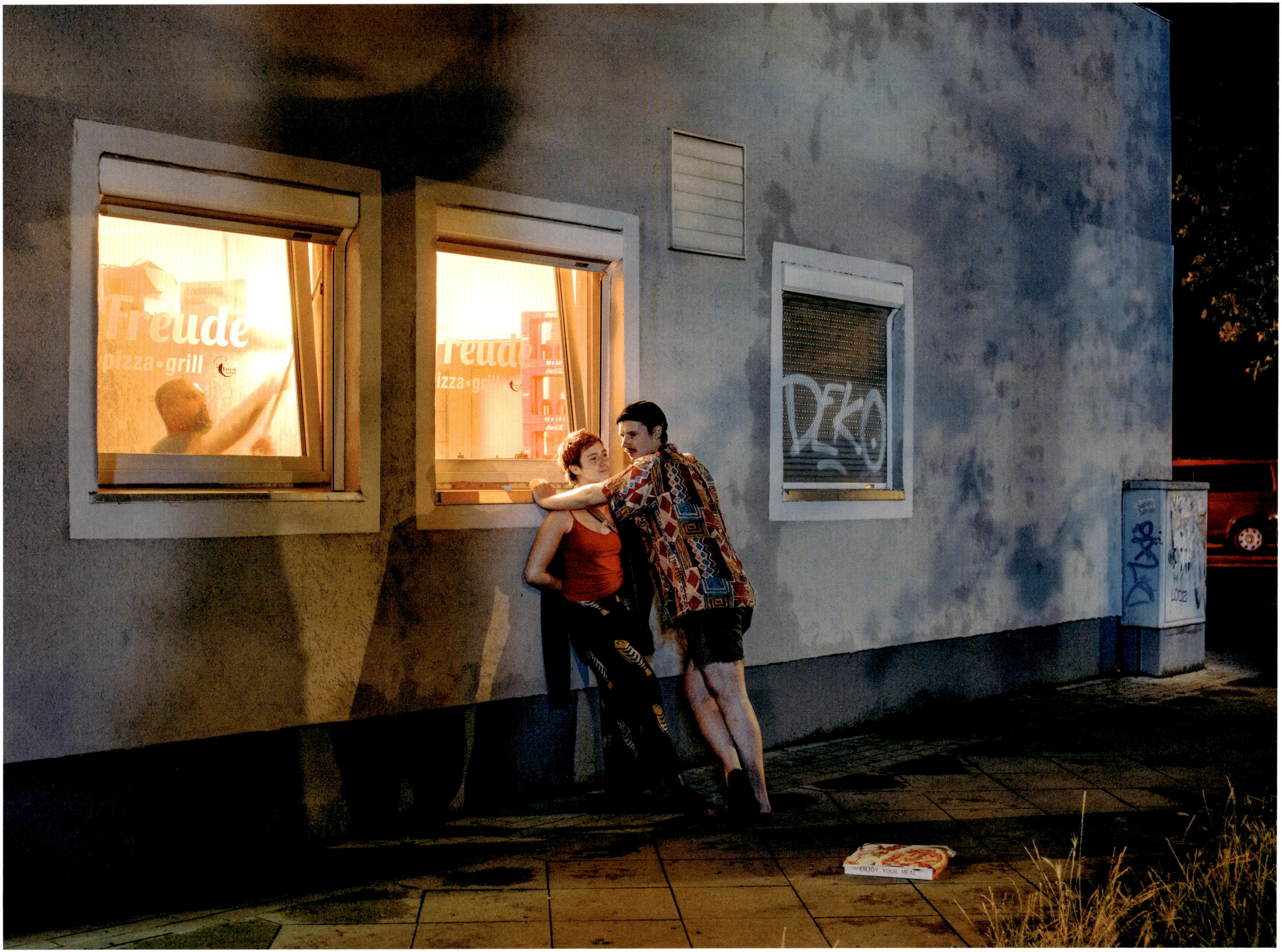

Freude
pizza • grill
DEKO
ENJOY YOUR MEAL

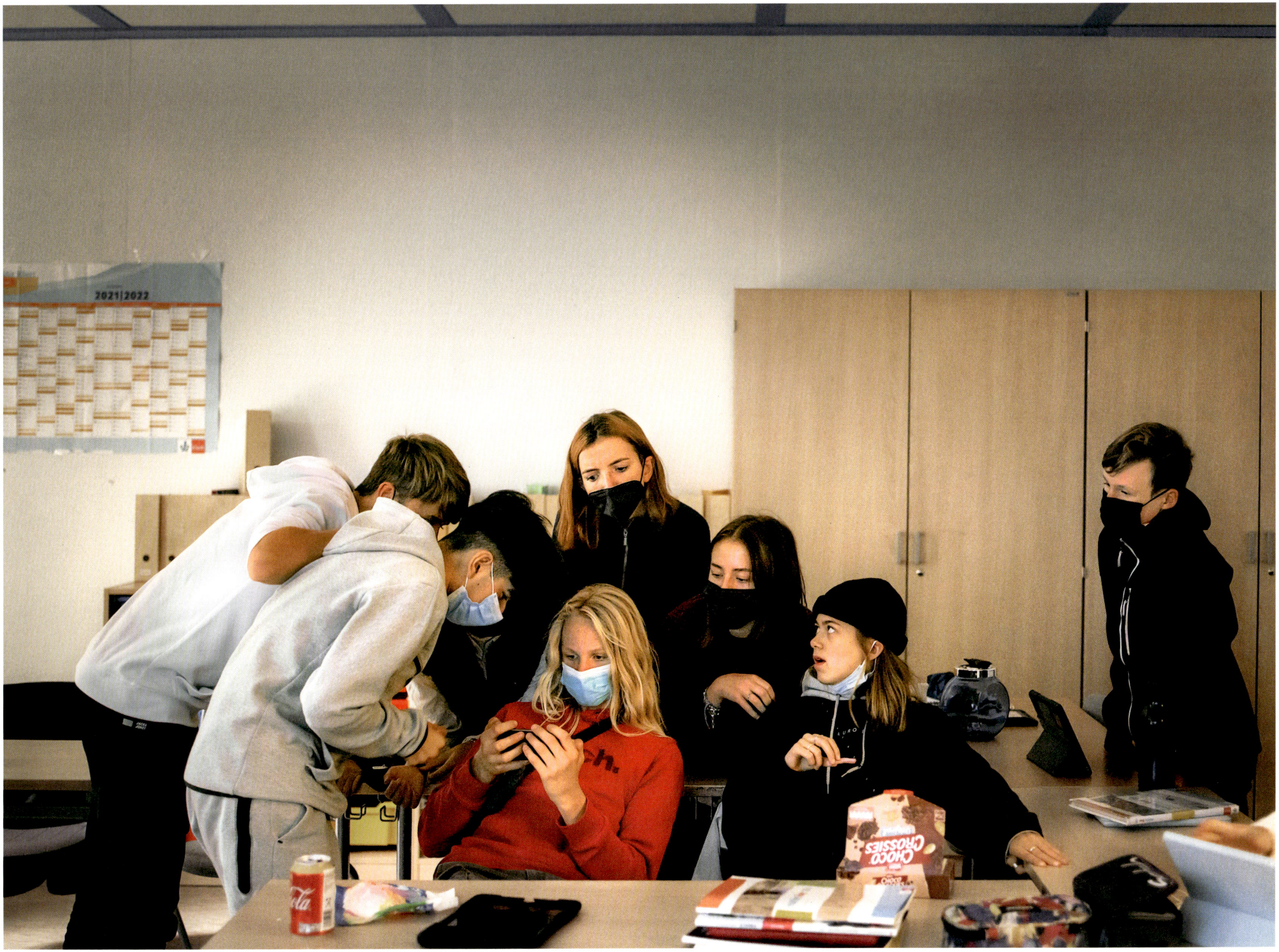
2021|2022

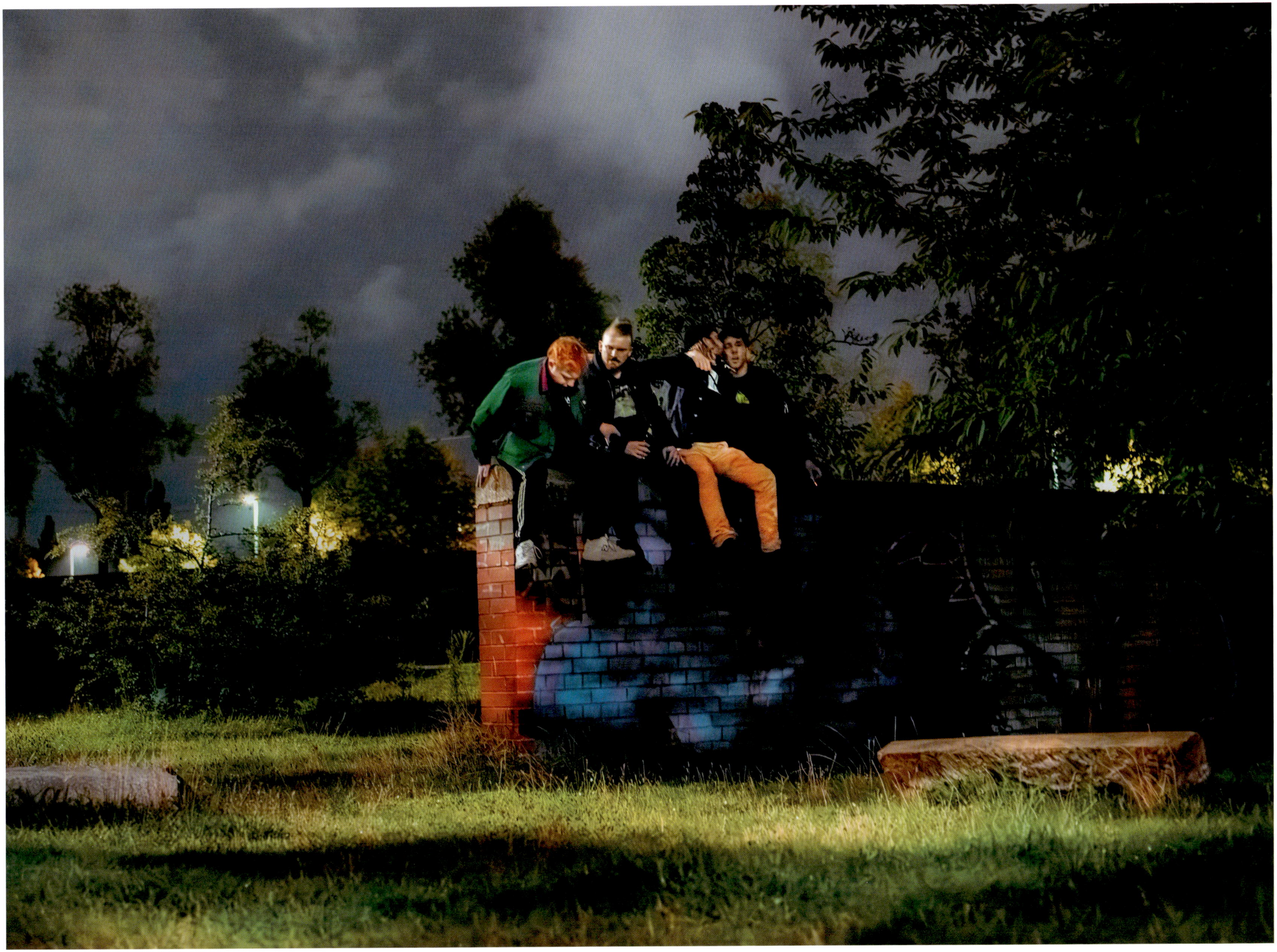

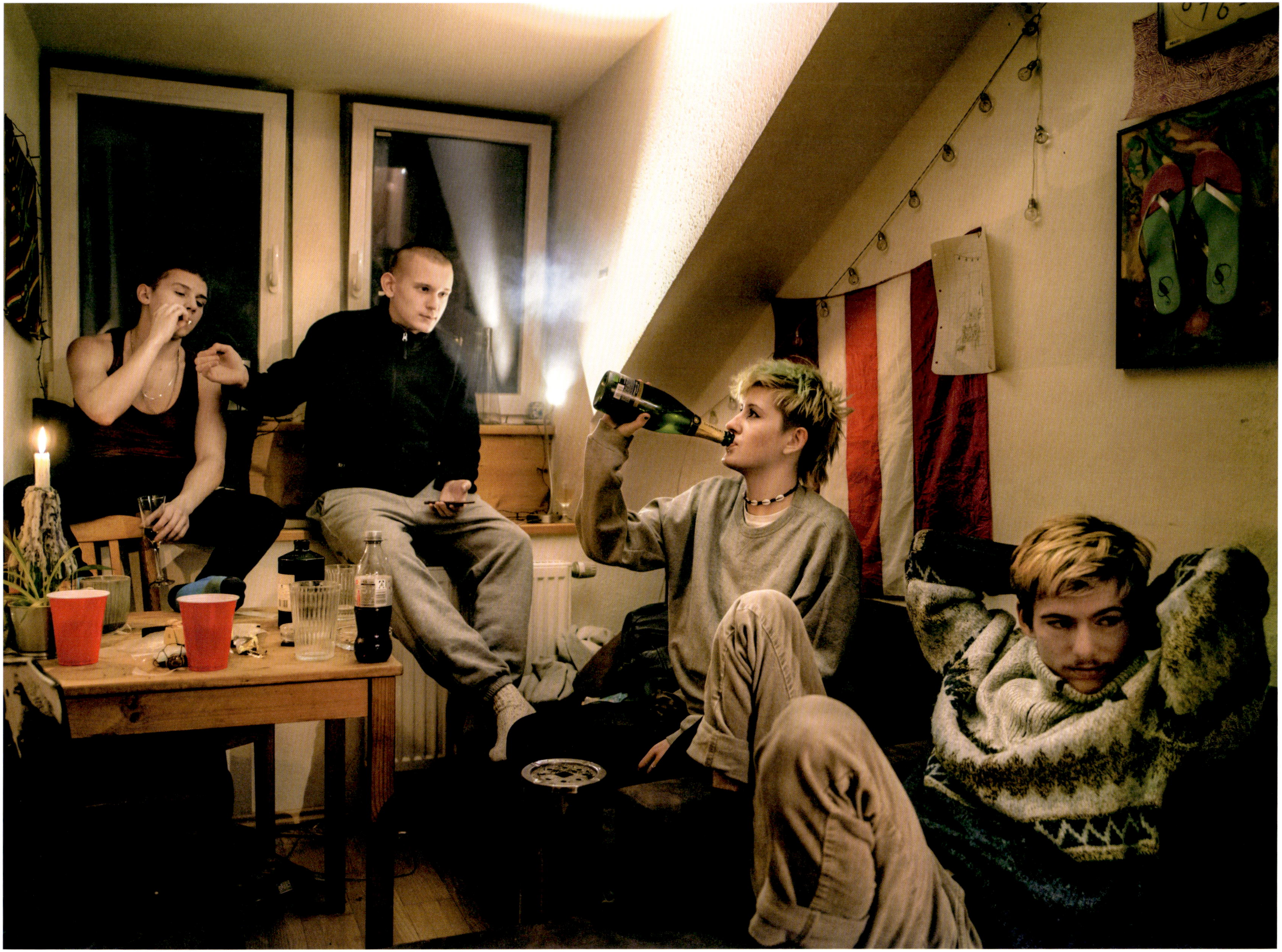

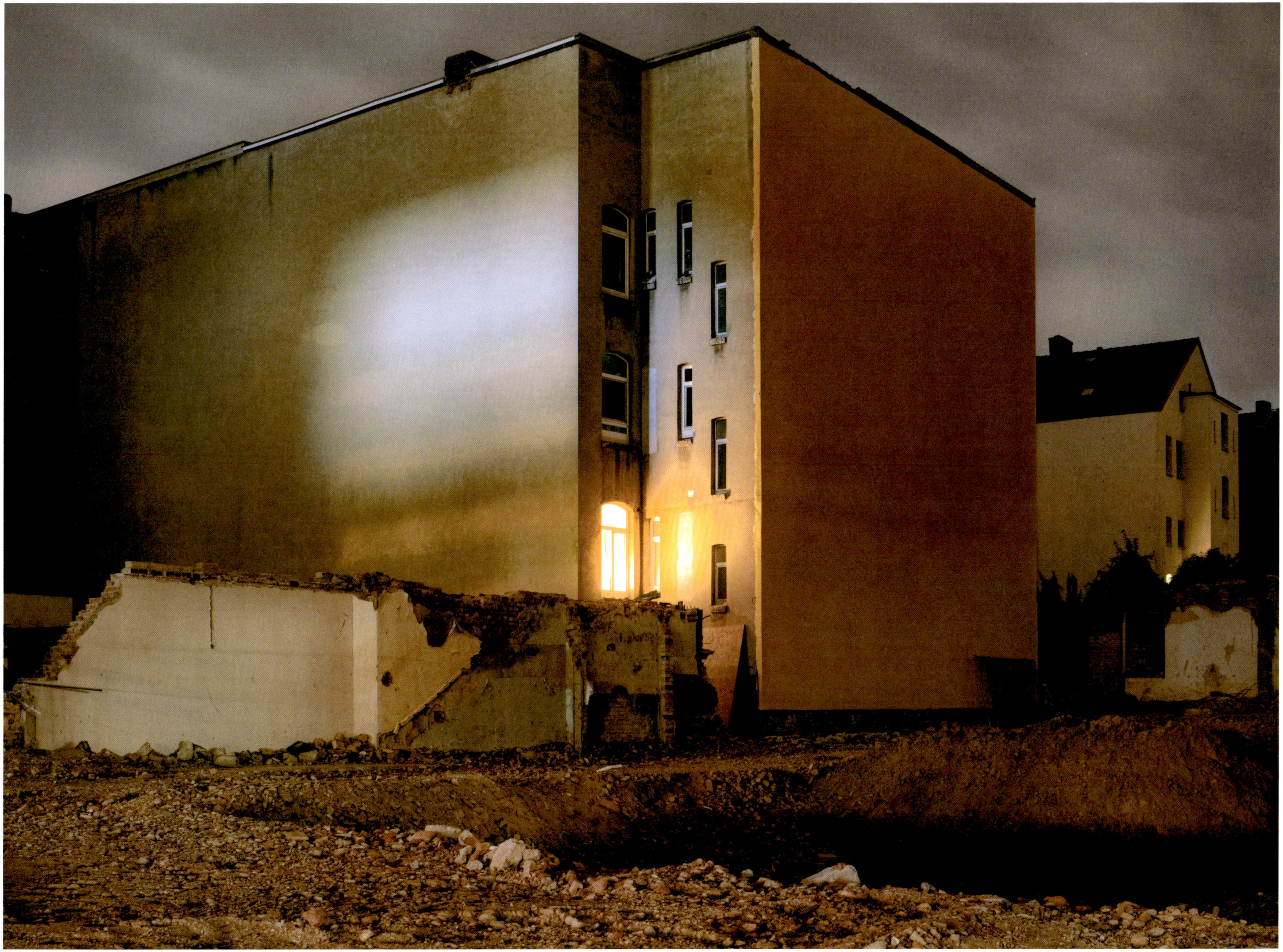

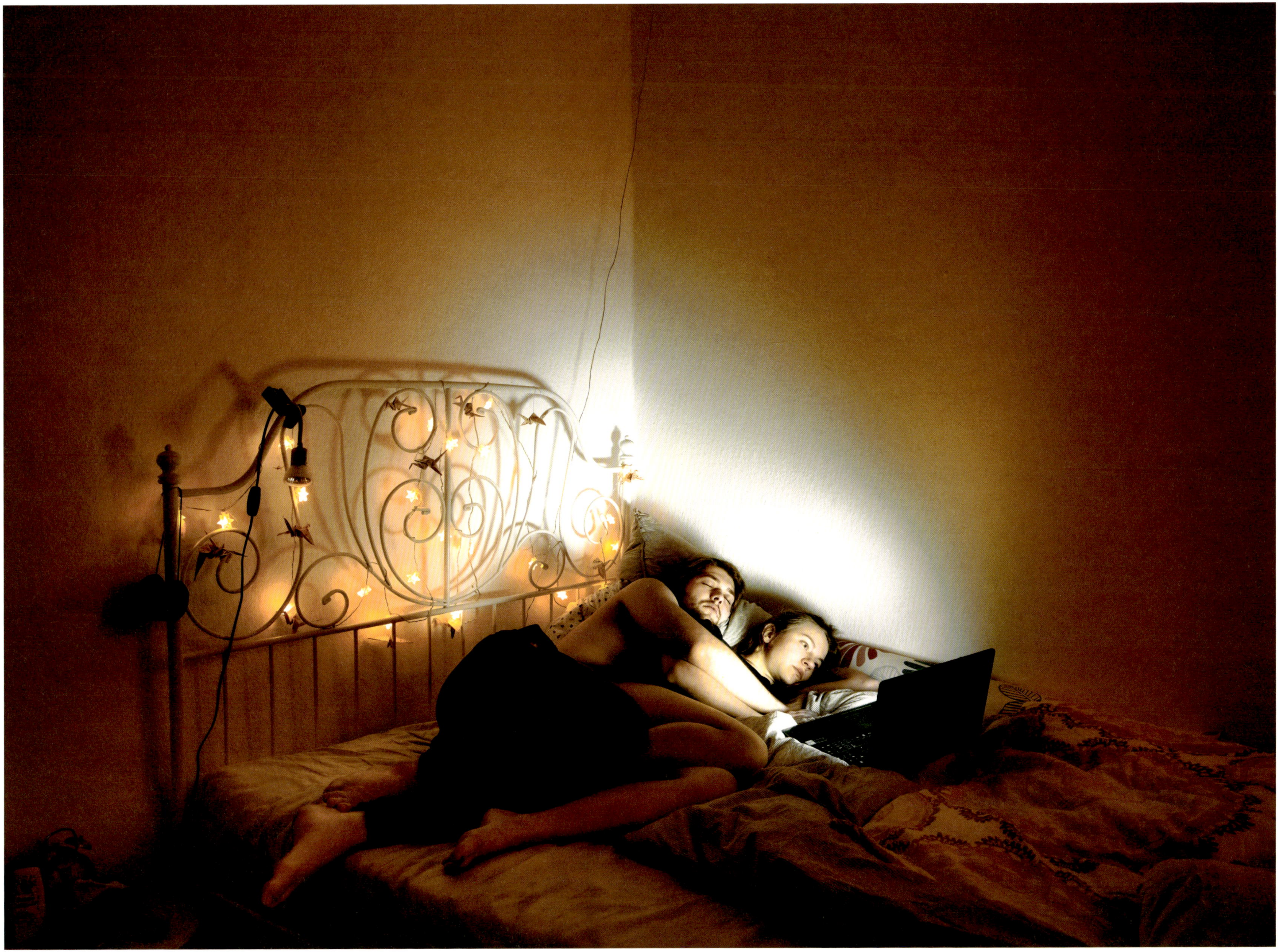

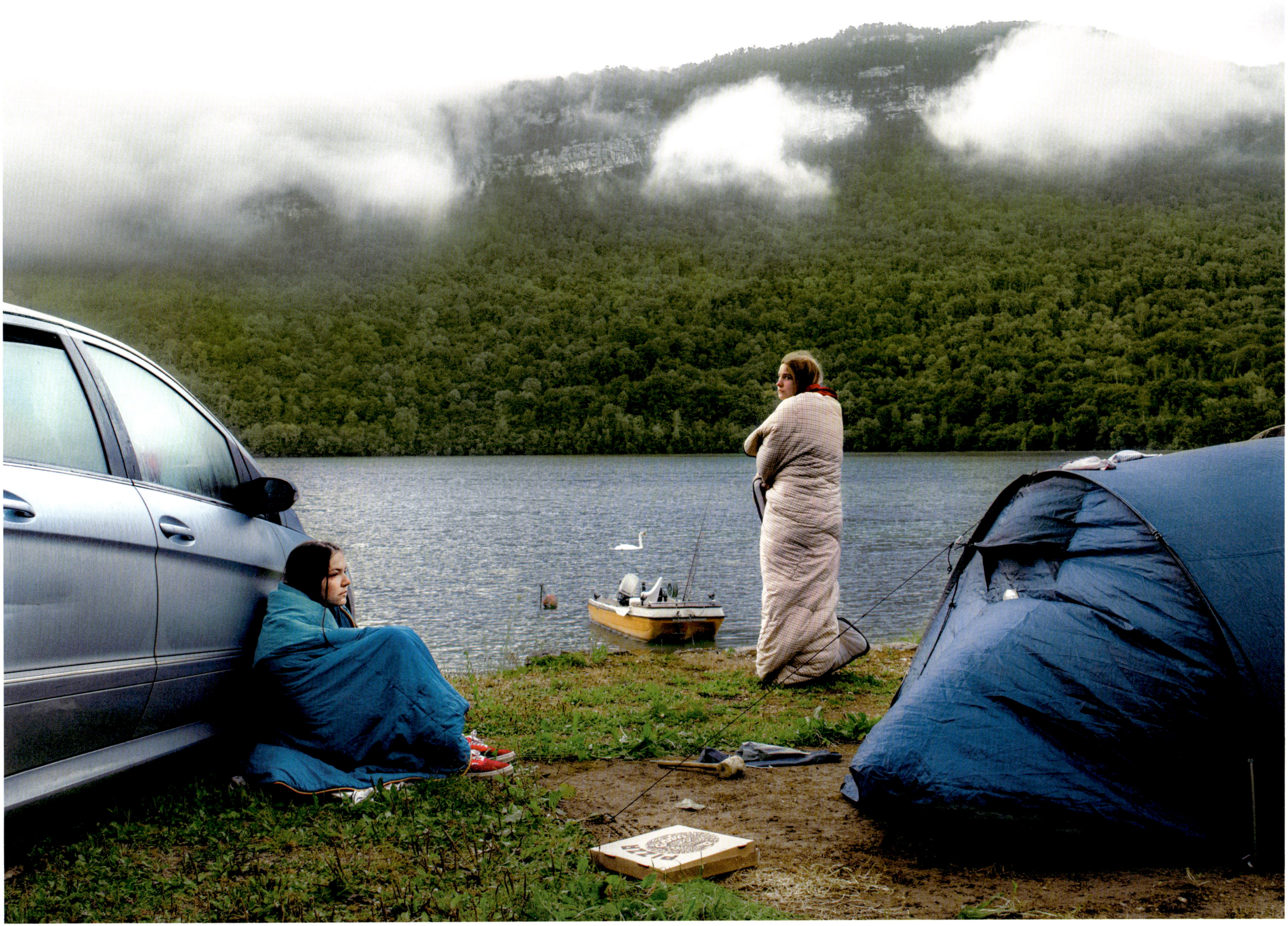

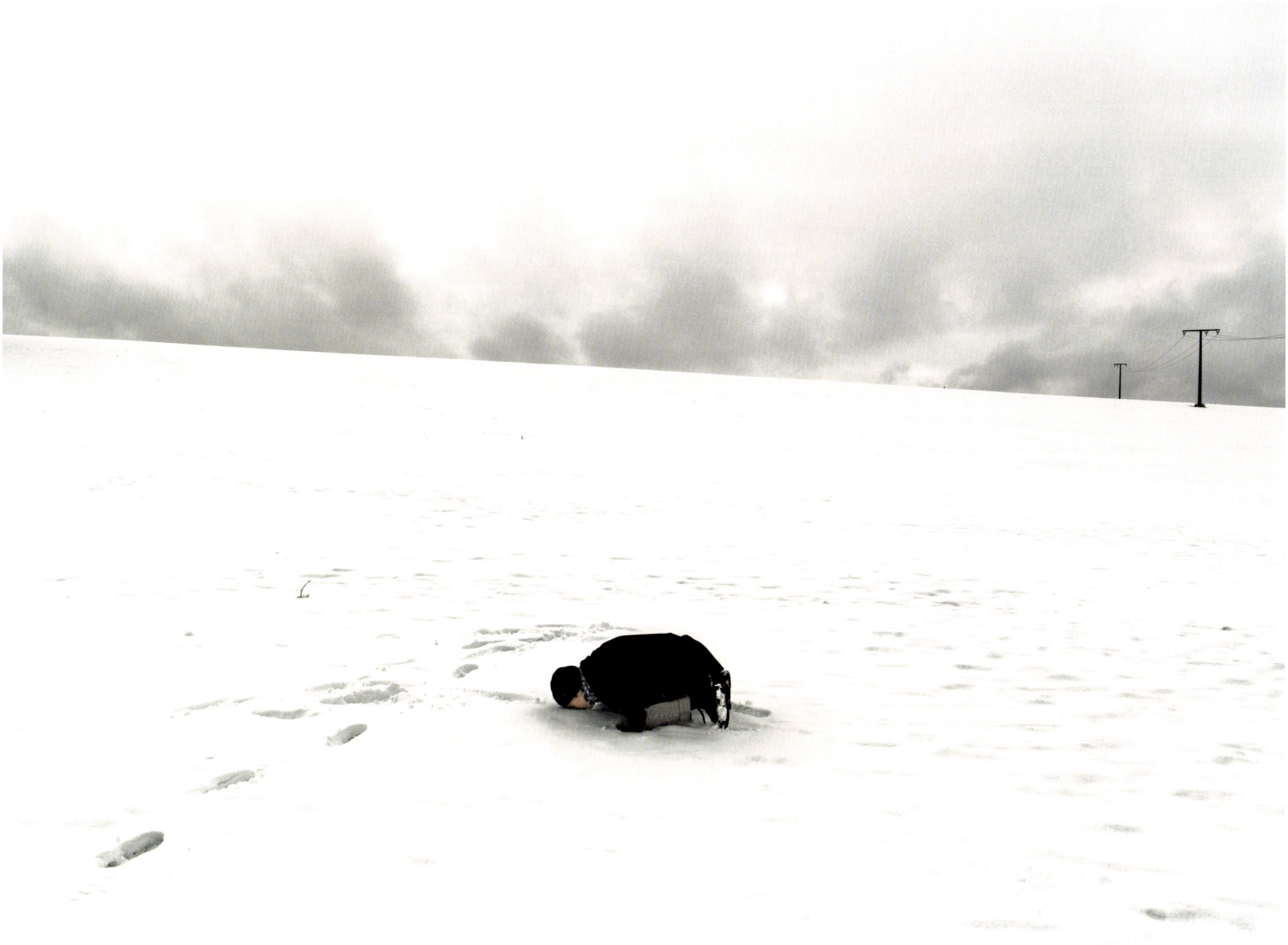

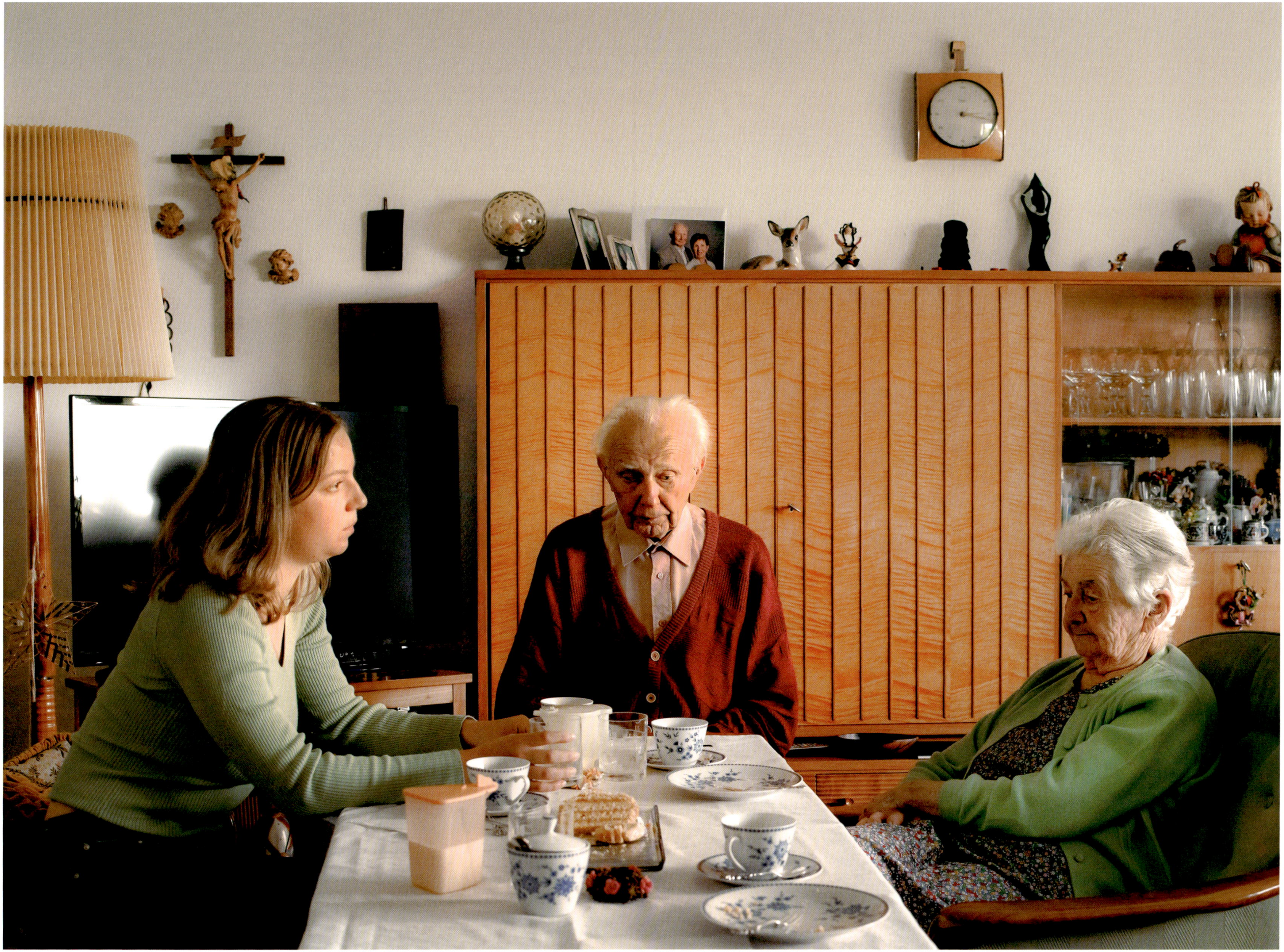

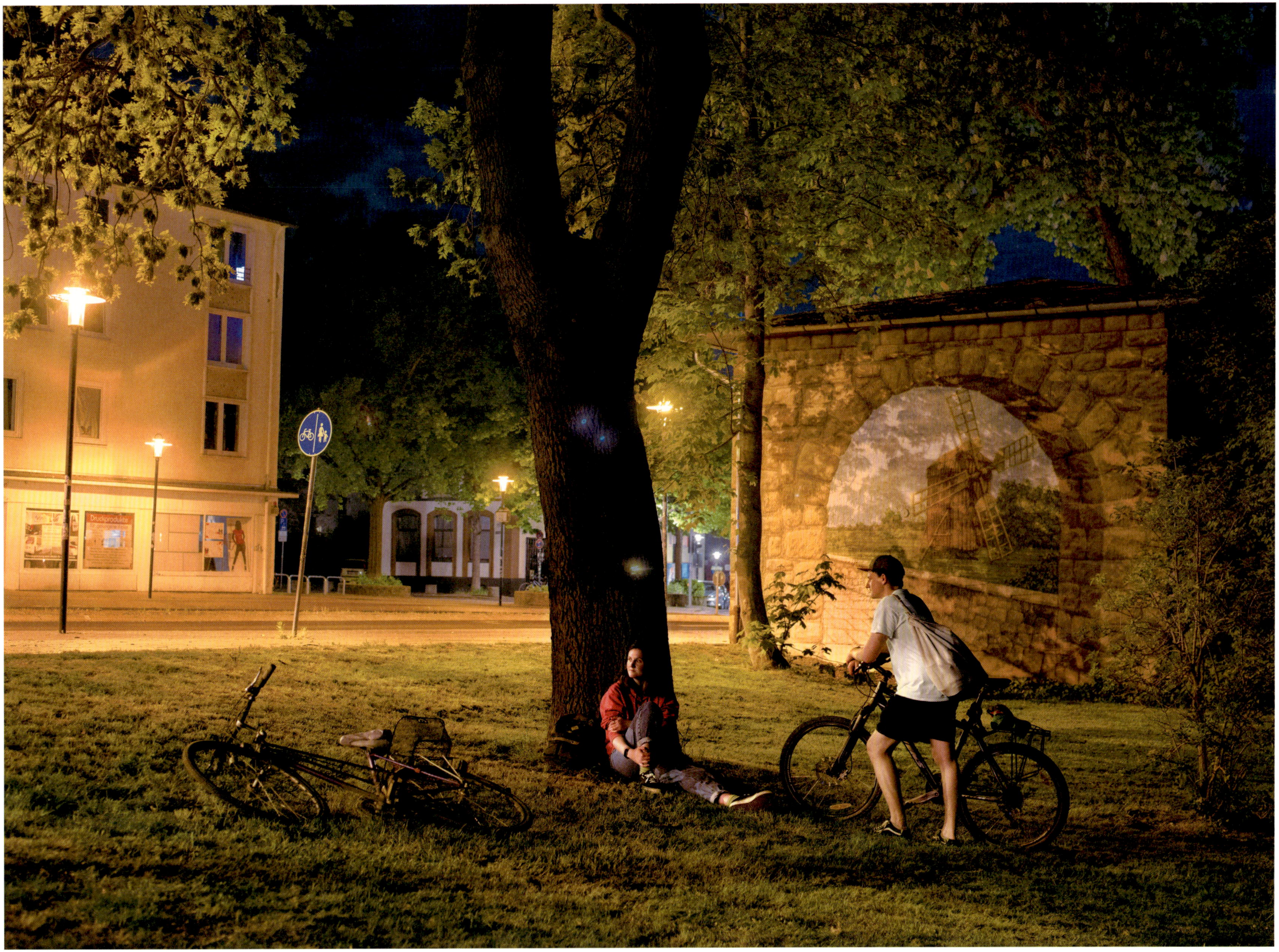

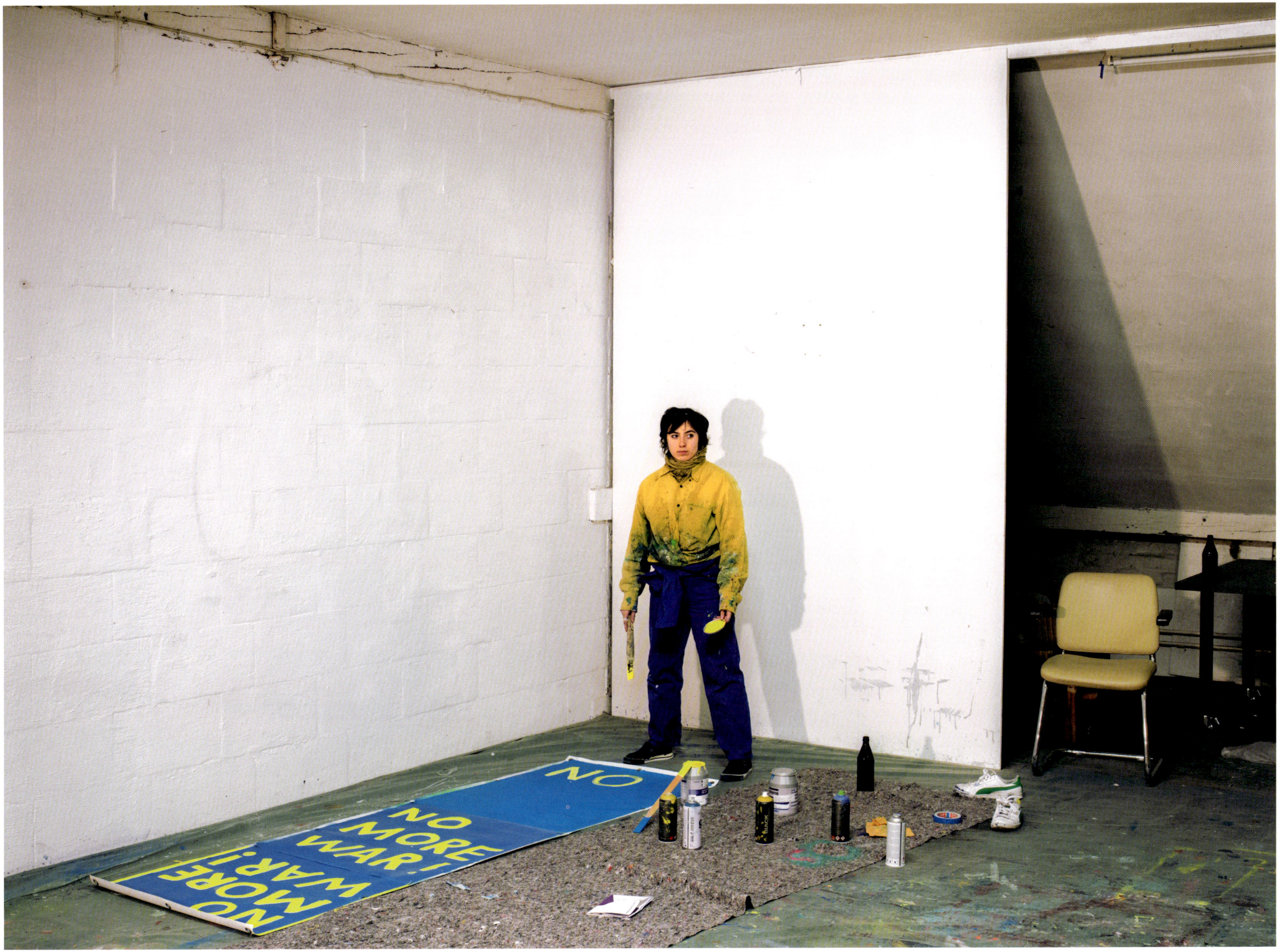
NO
MORE
WAR!
NO
MORE
WAR!
NO

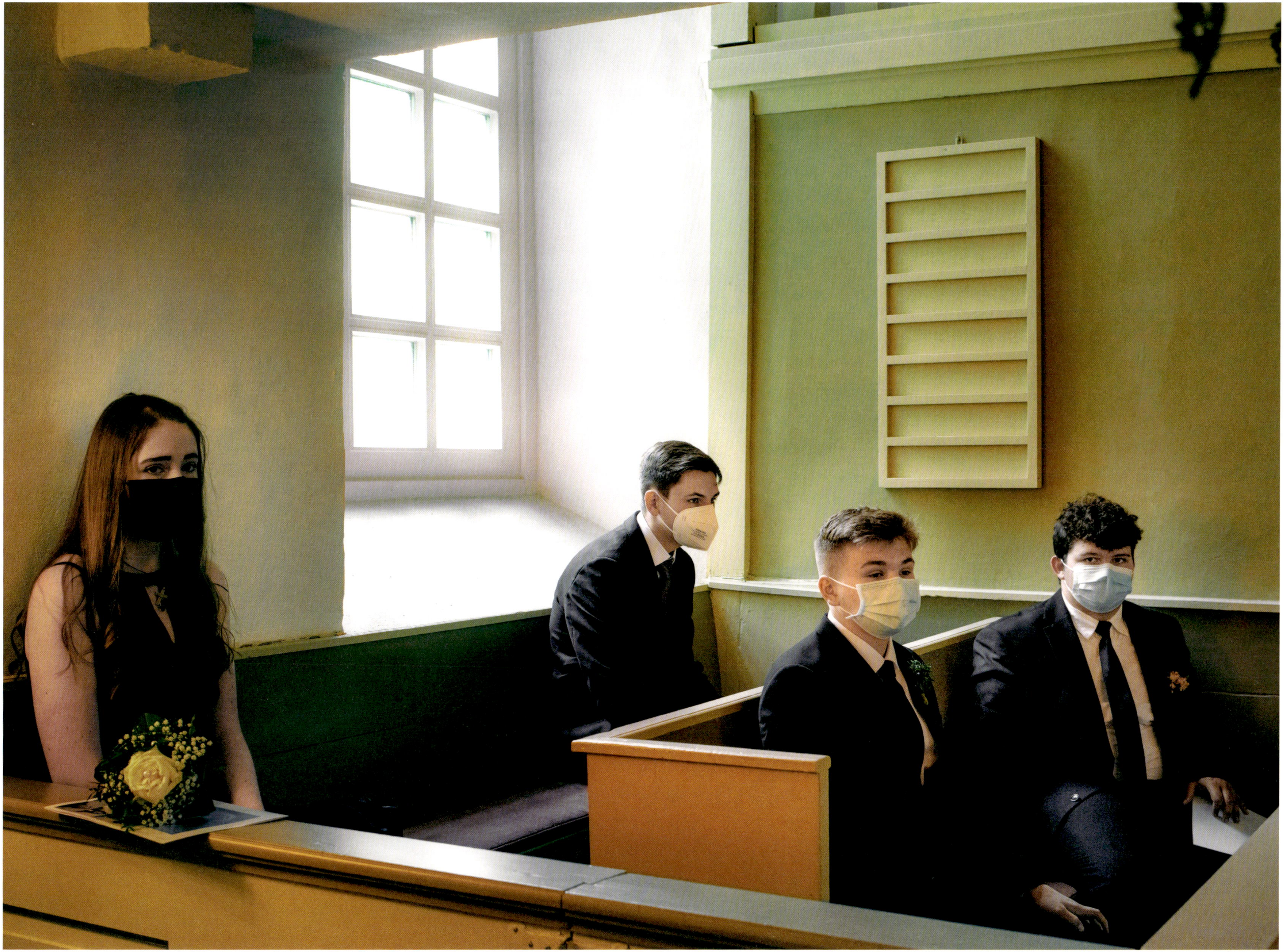

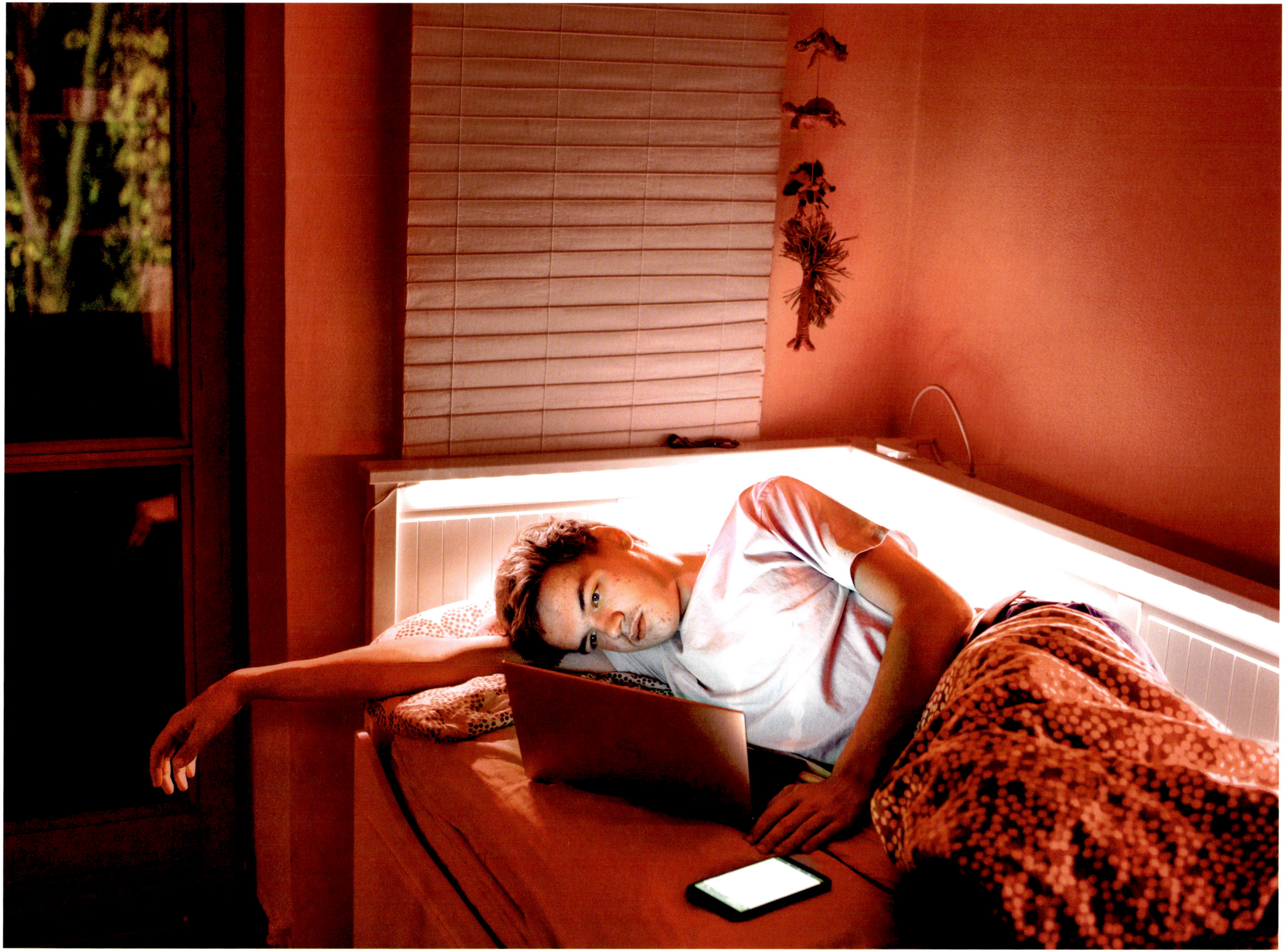

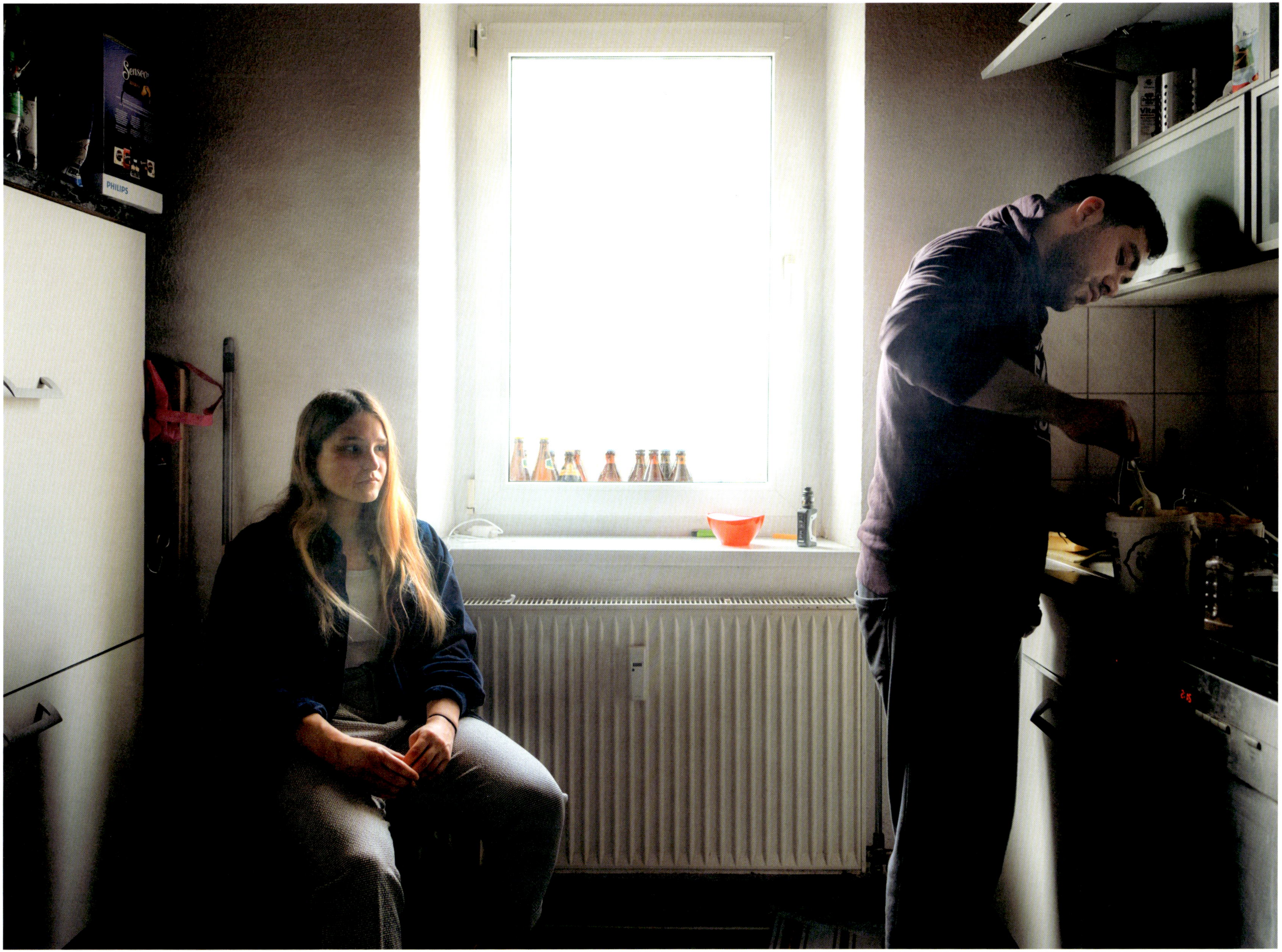
Senseo
PHILIPS

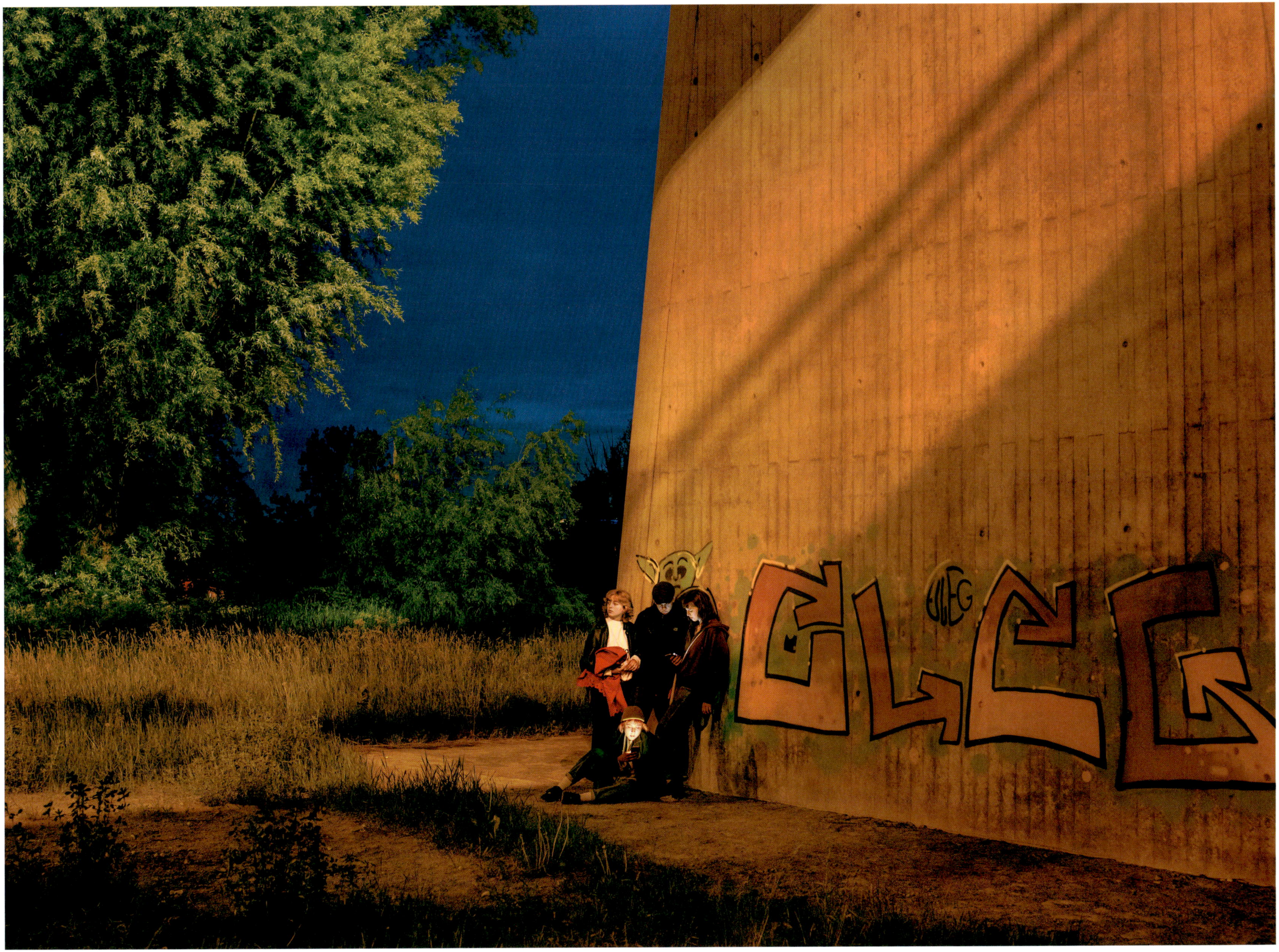

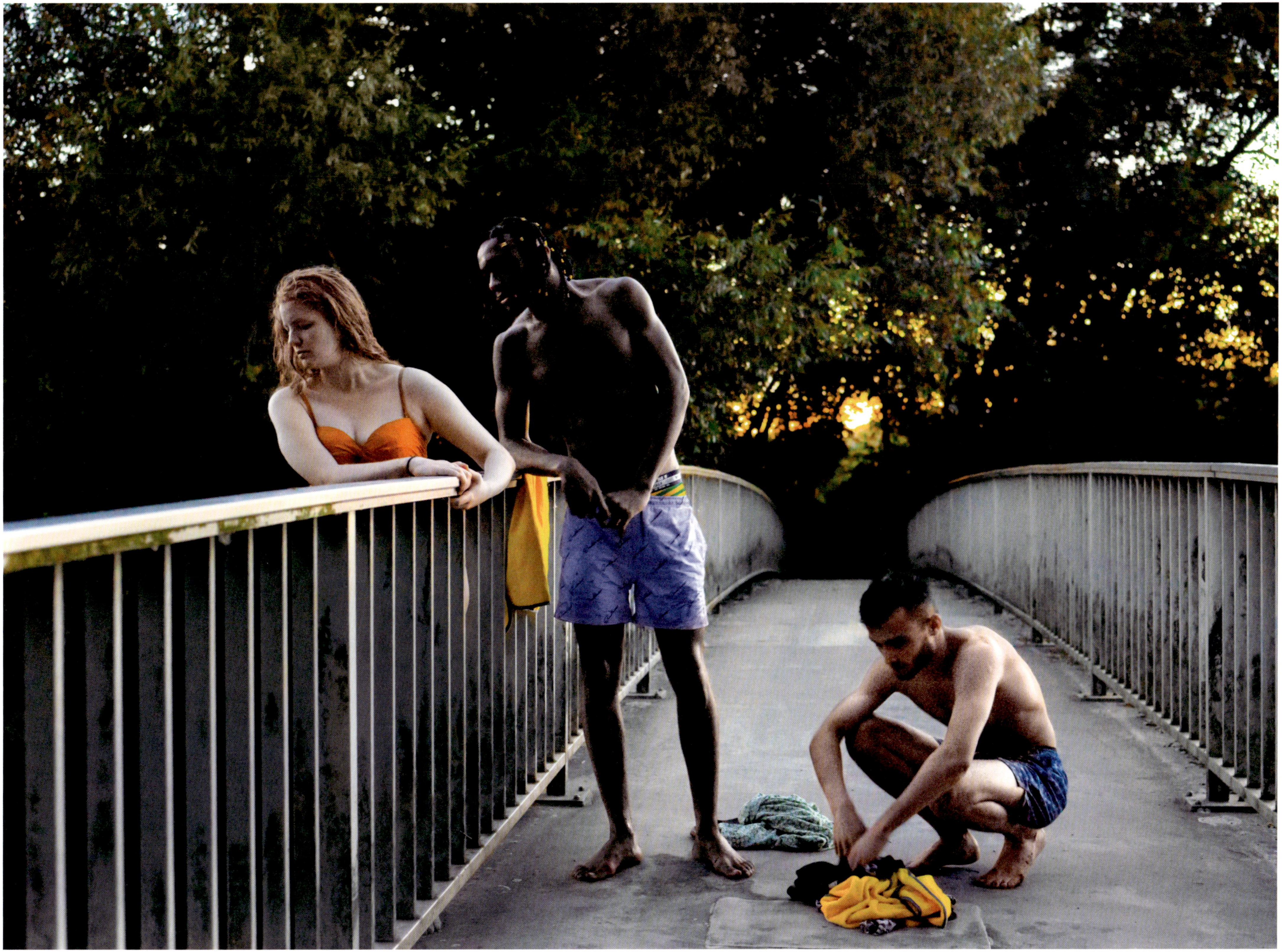

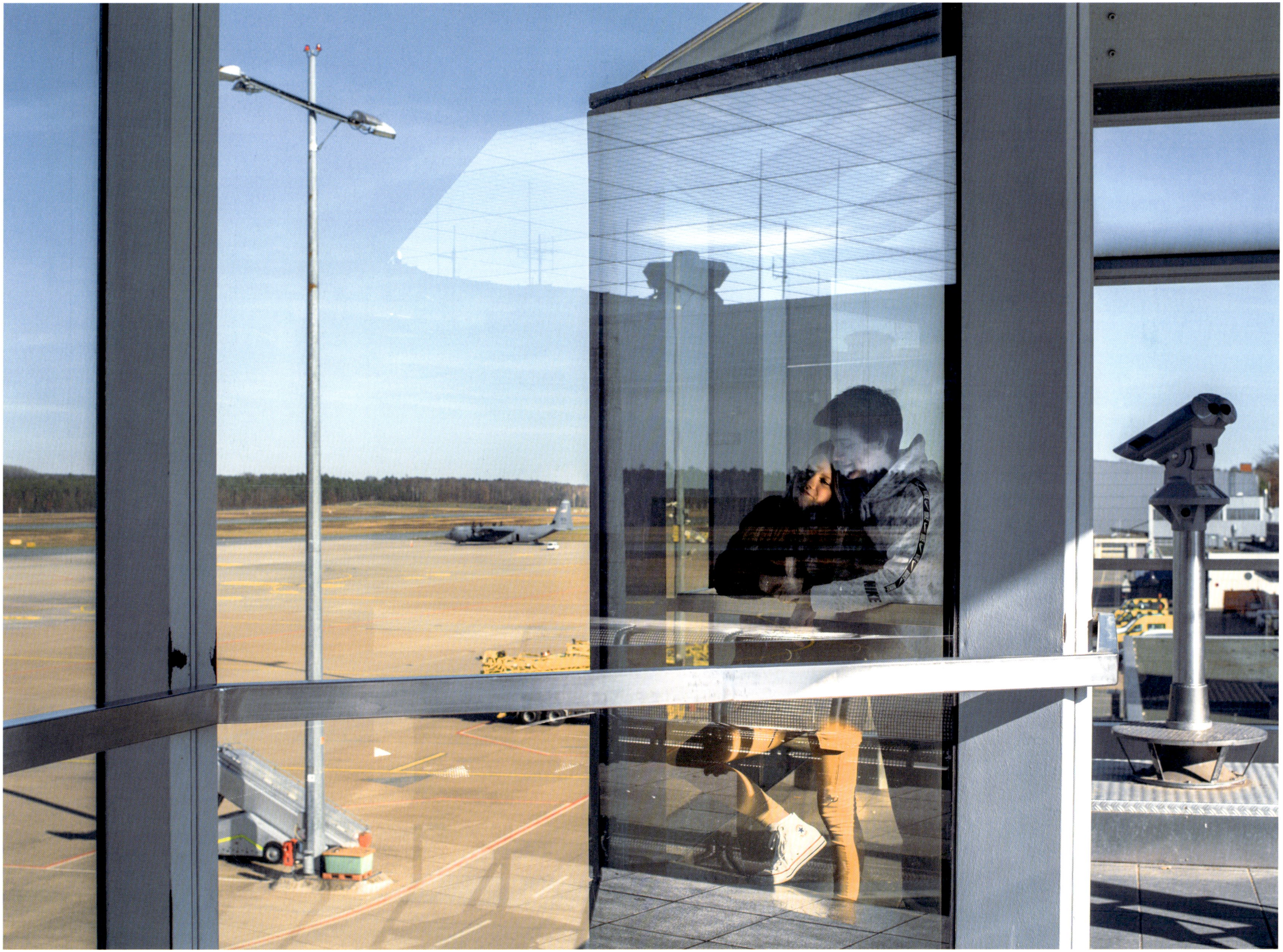

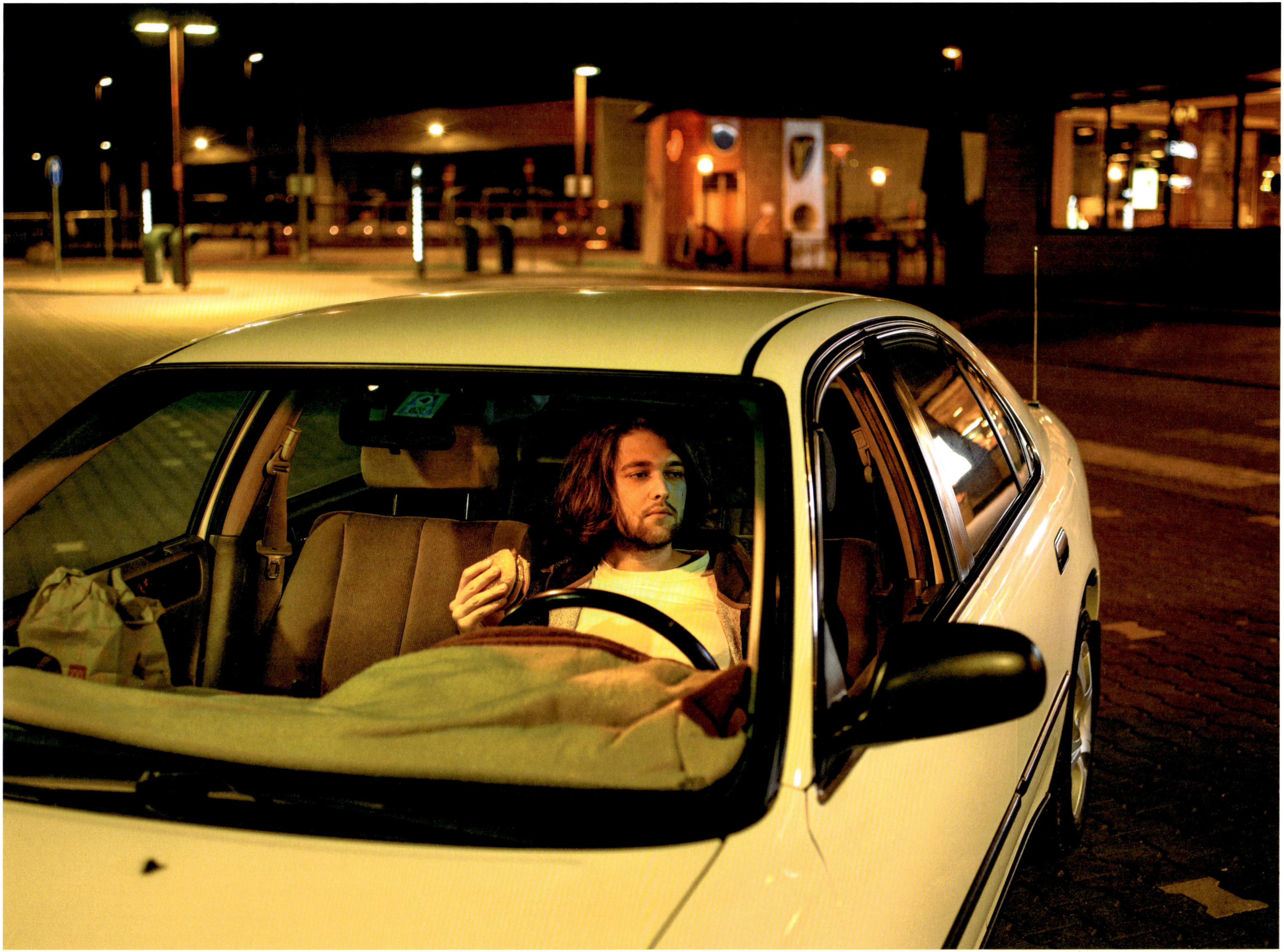

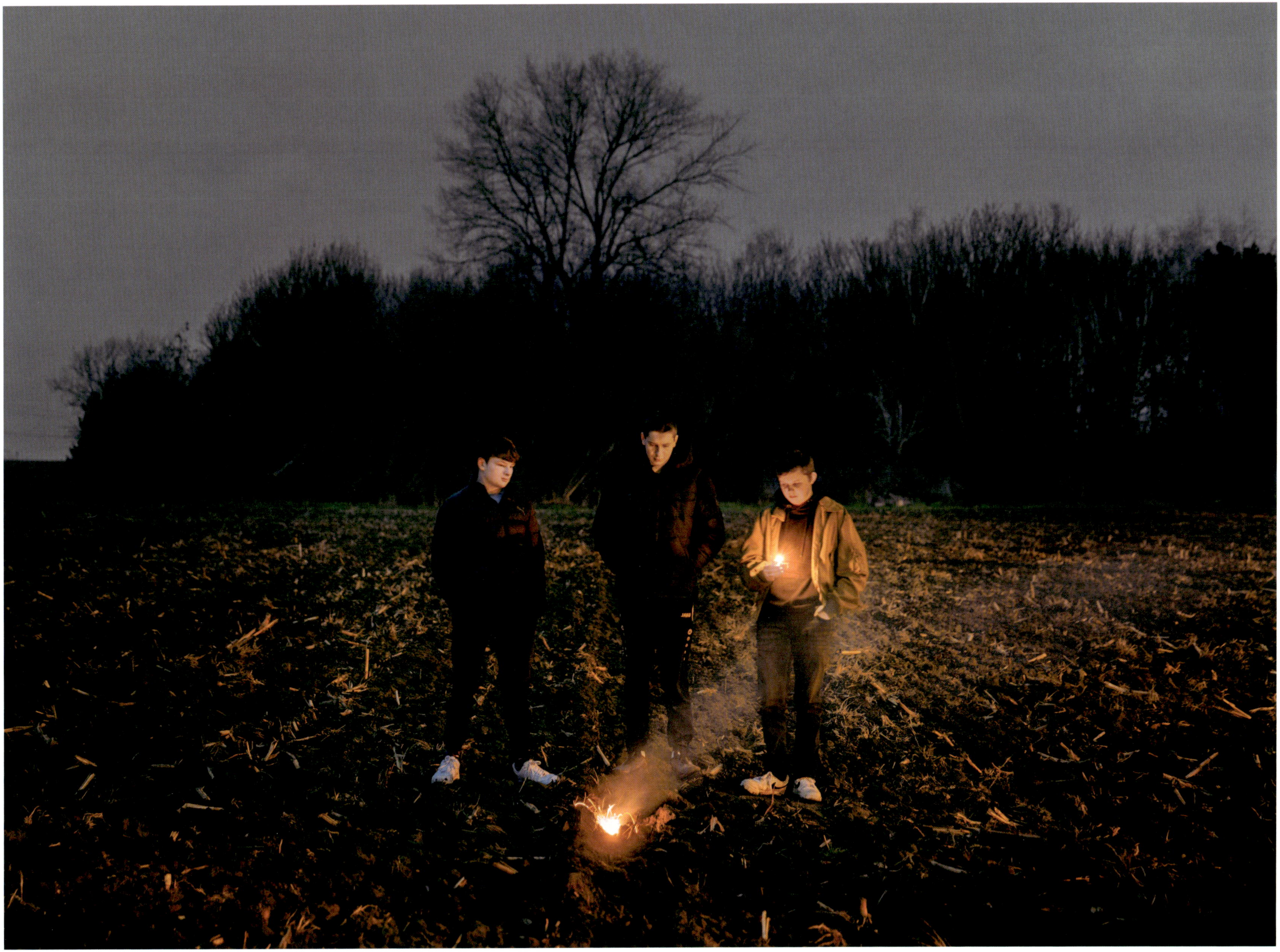

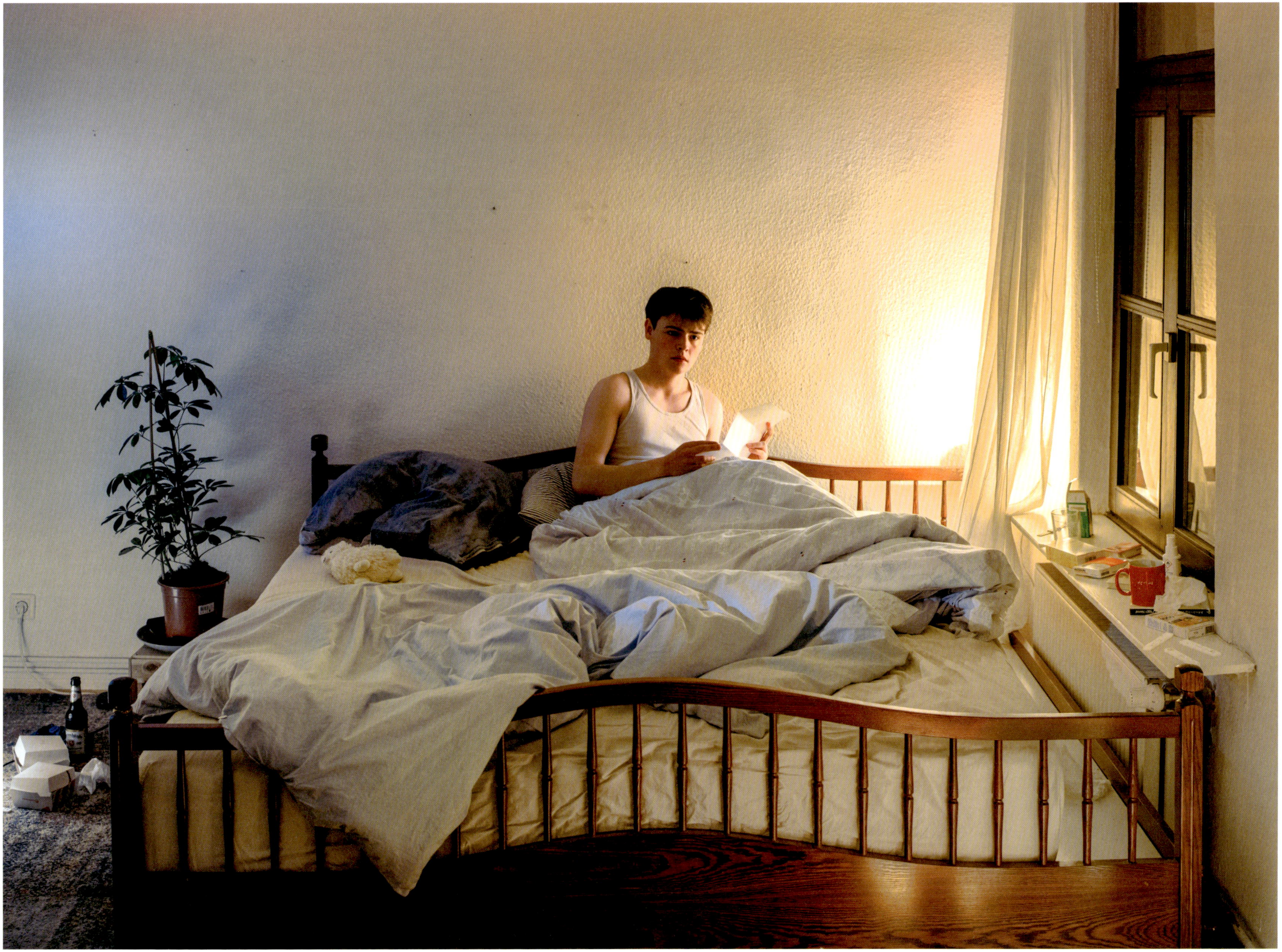

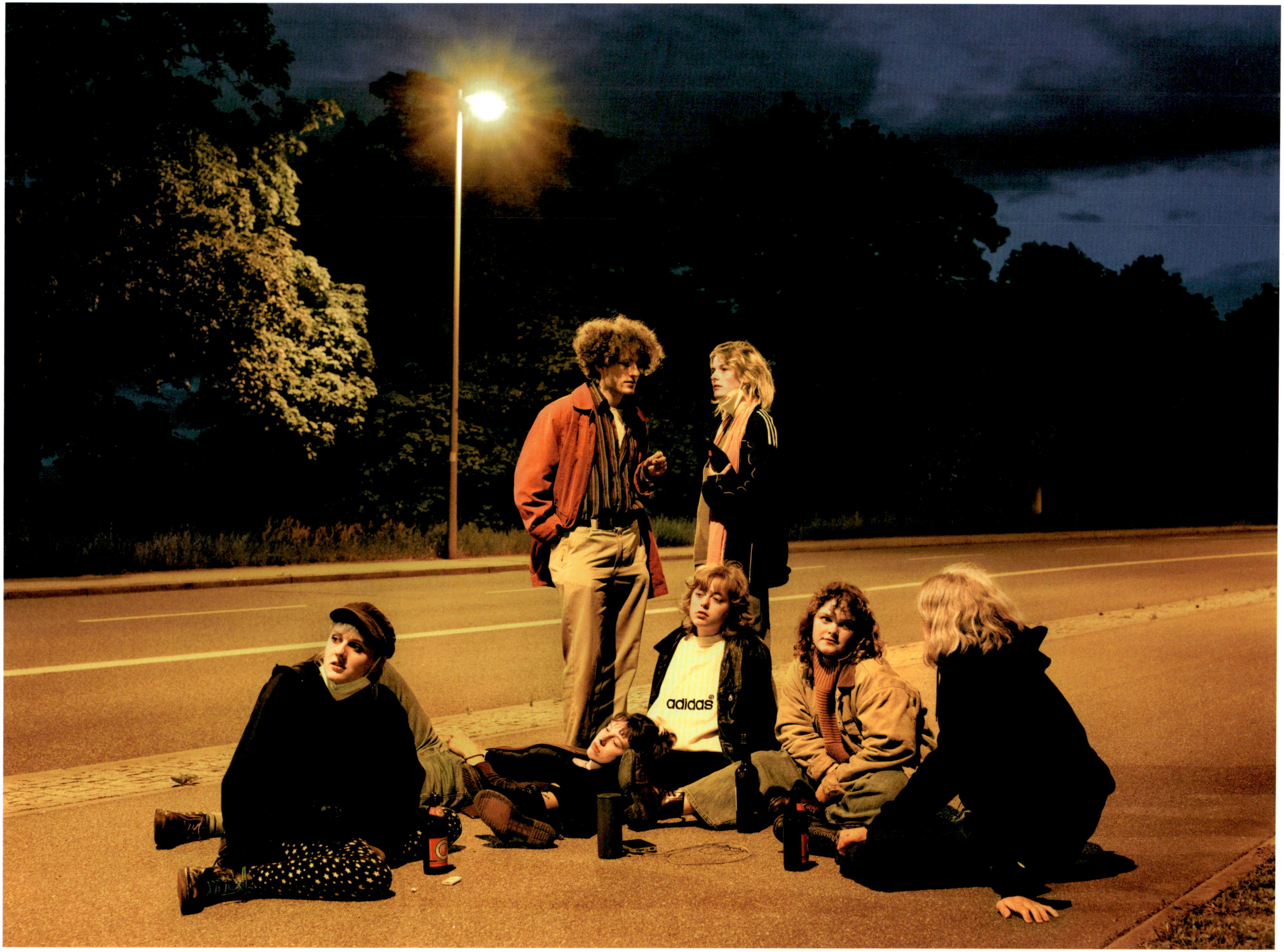
adidas

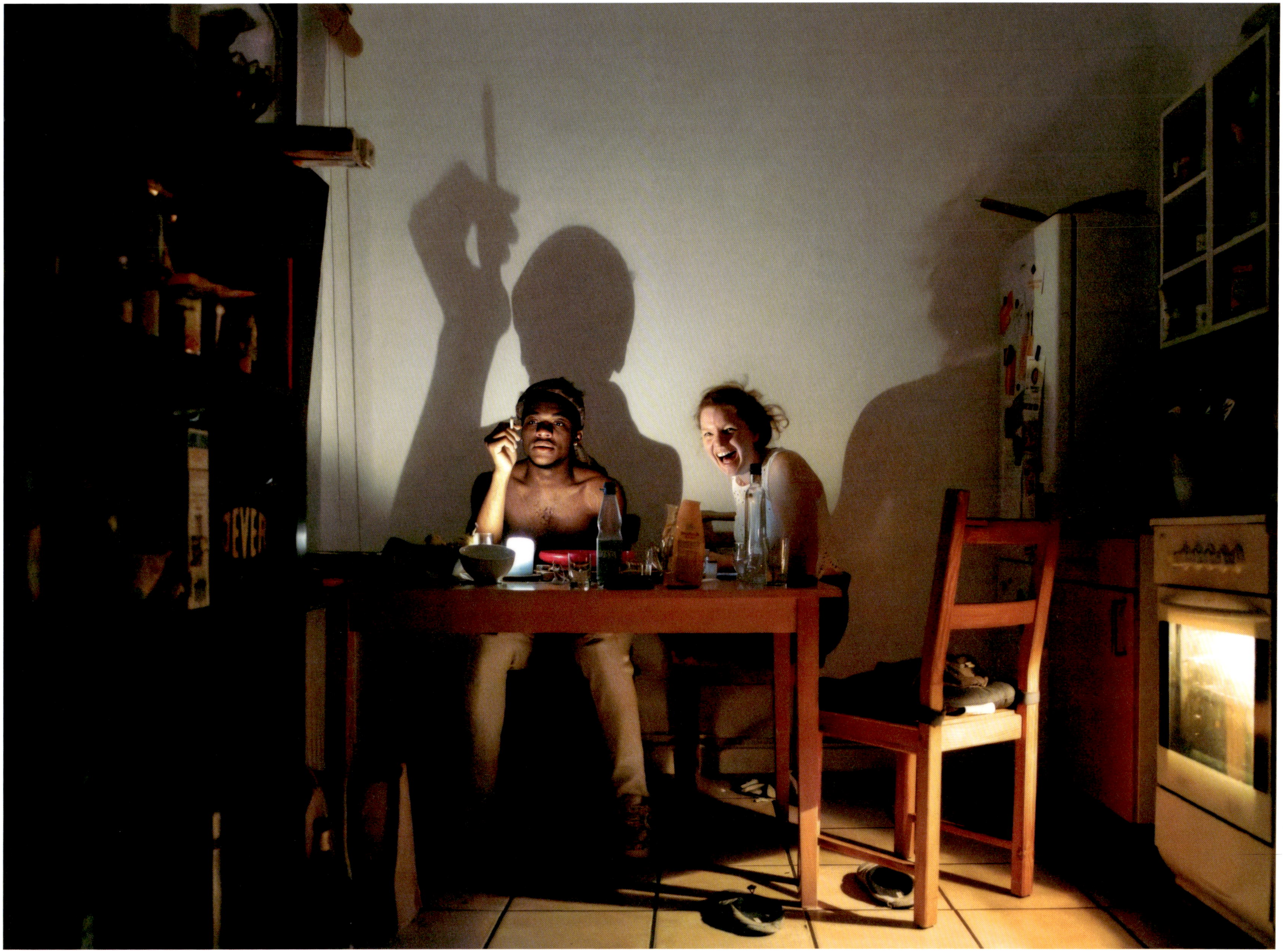
JEVER

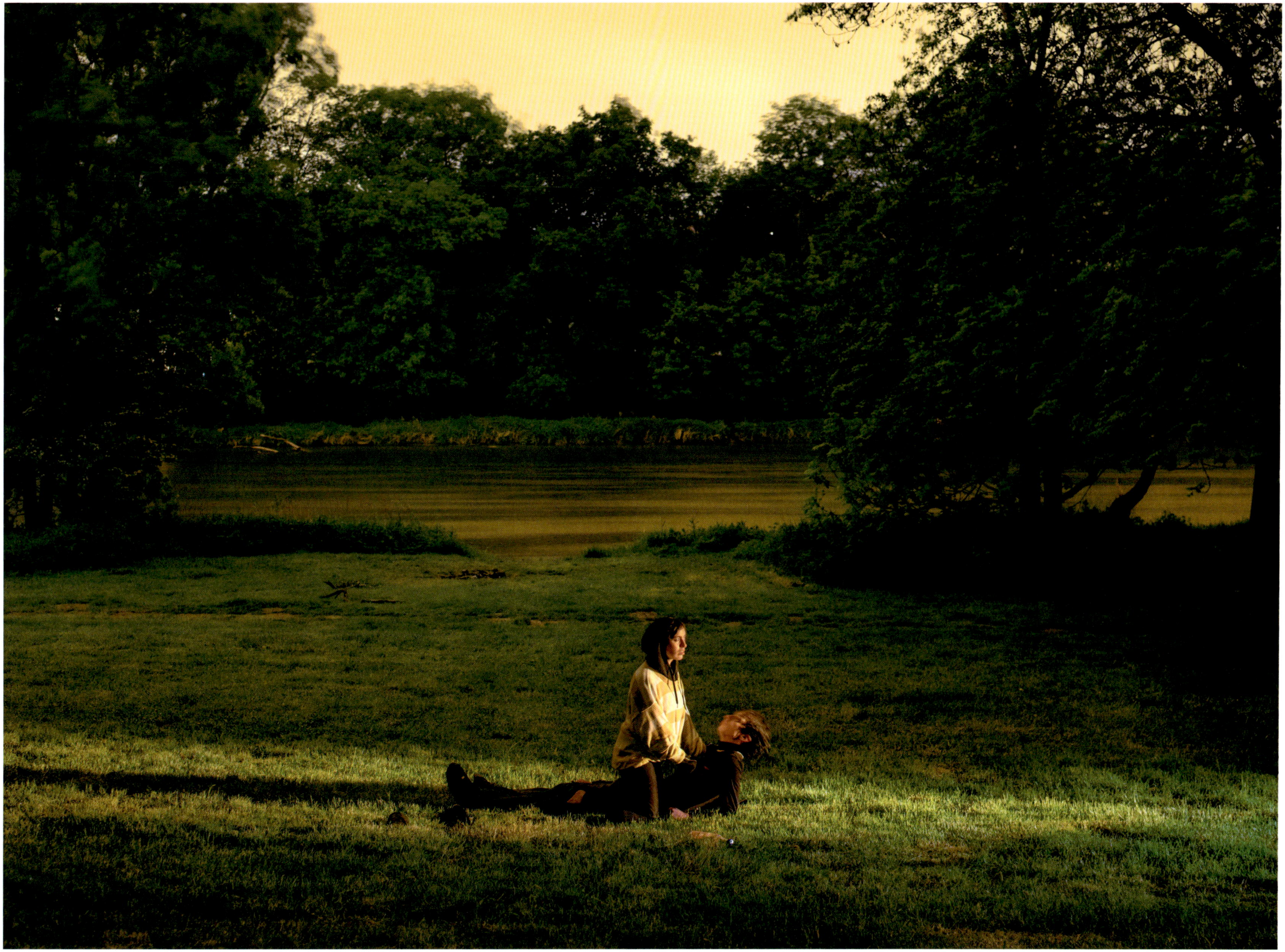

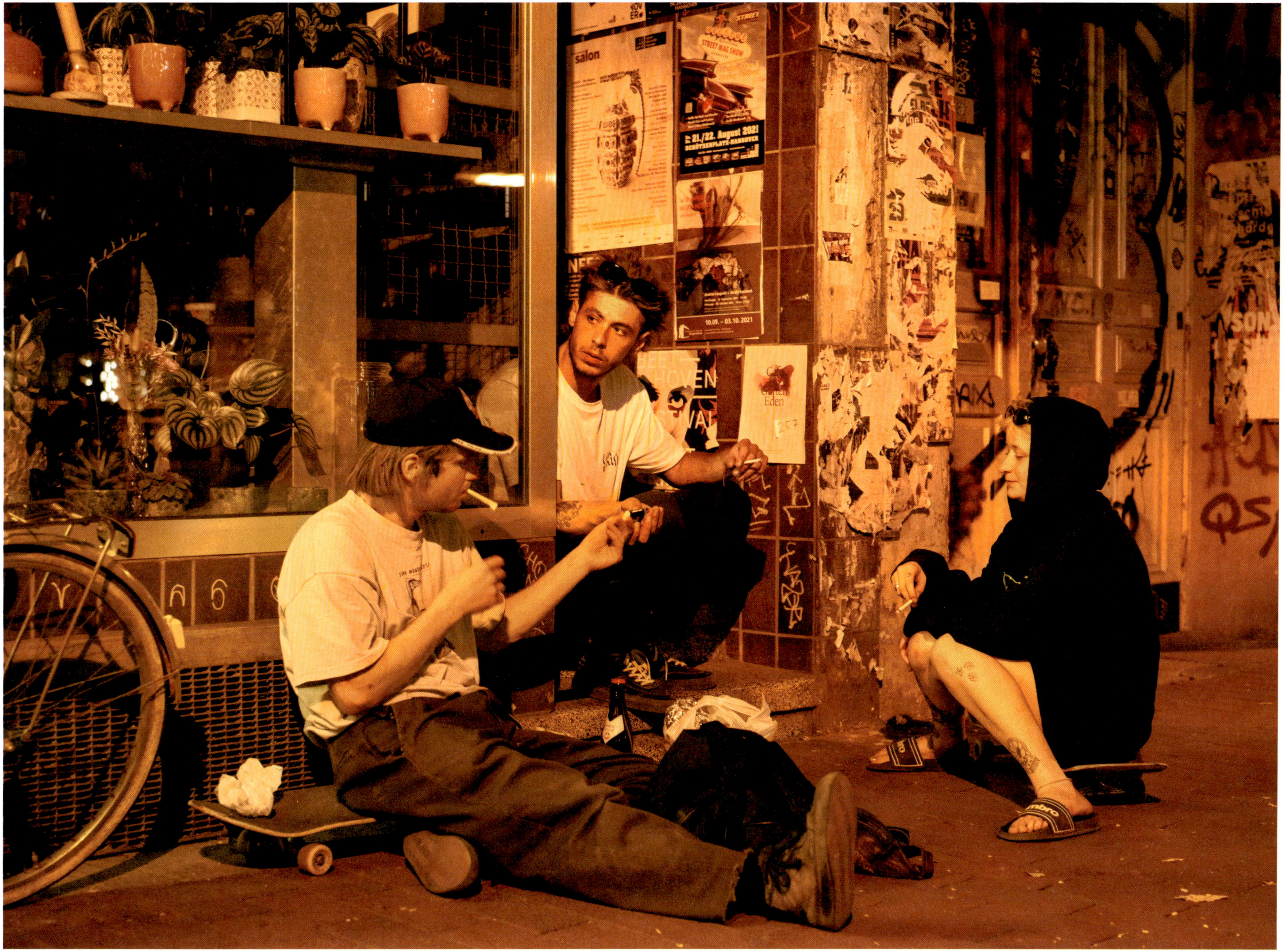
salon
STREET MAG SHOW
21./22. August 2021
Eden
257

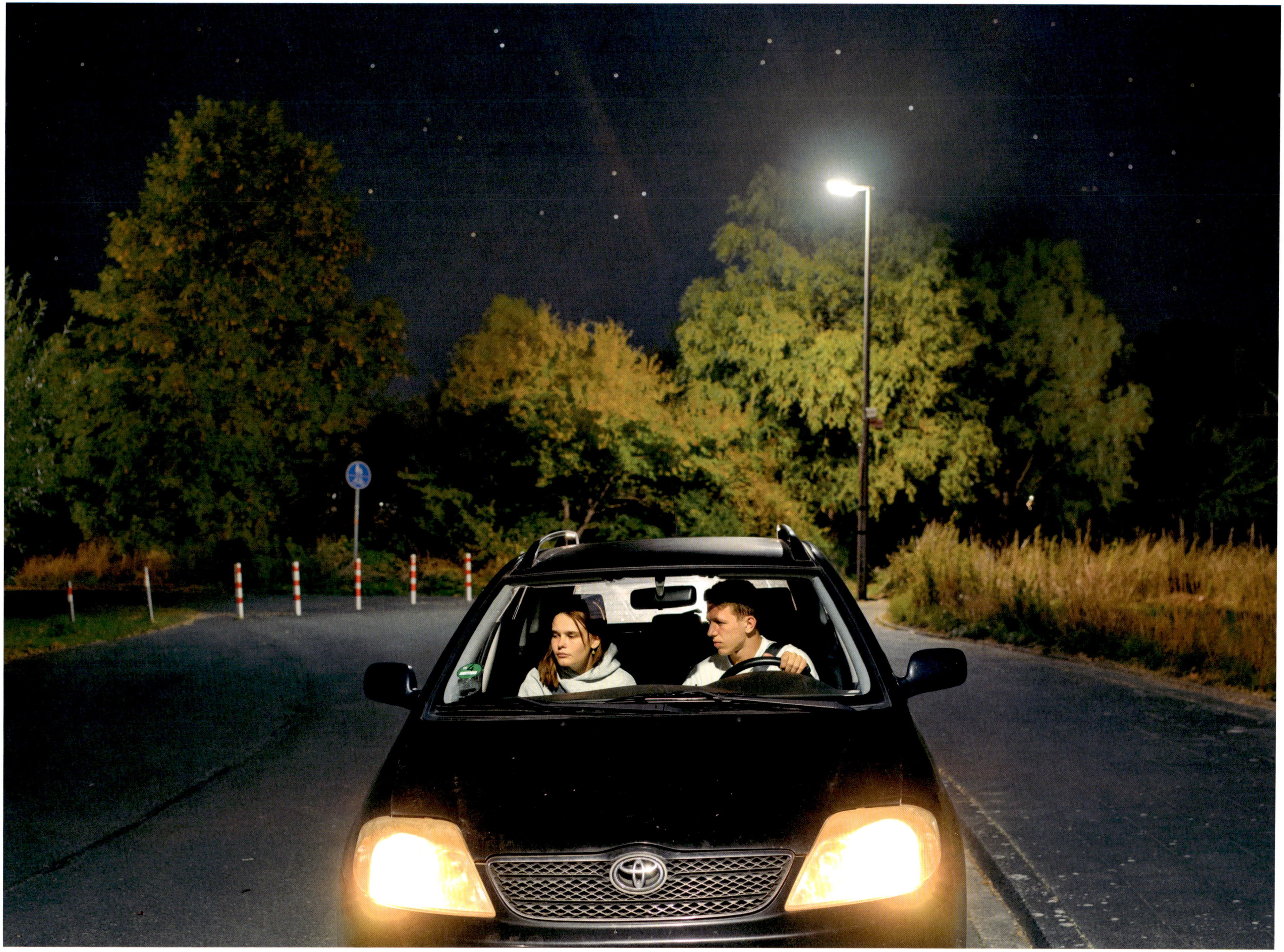

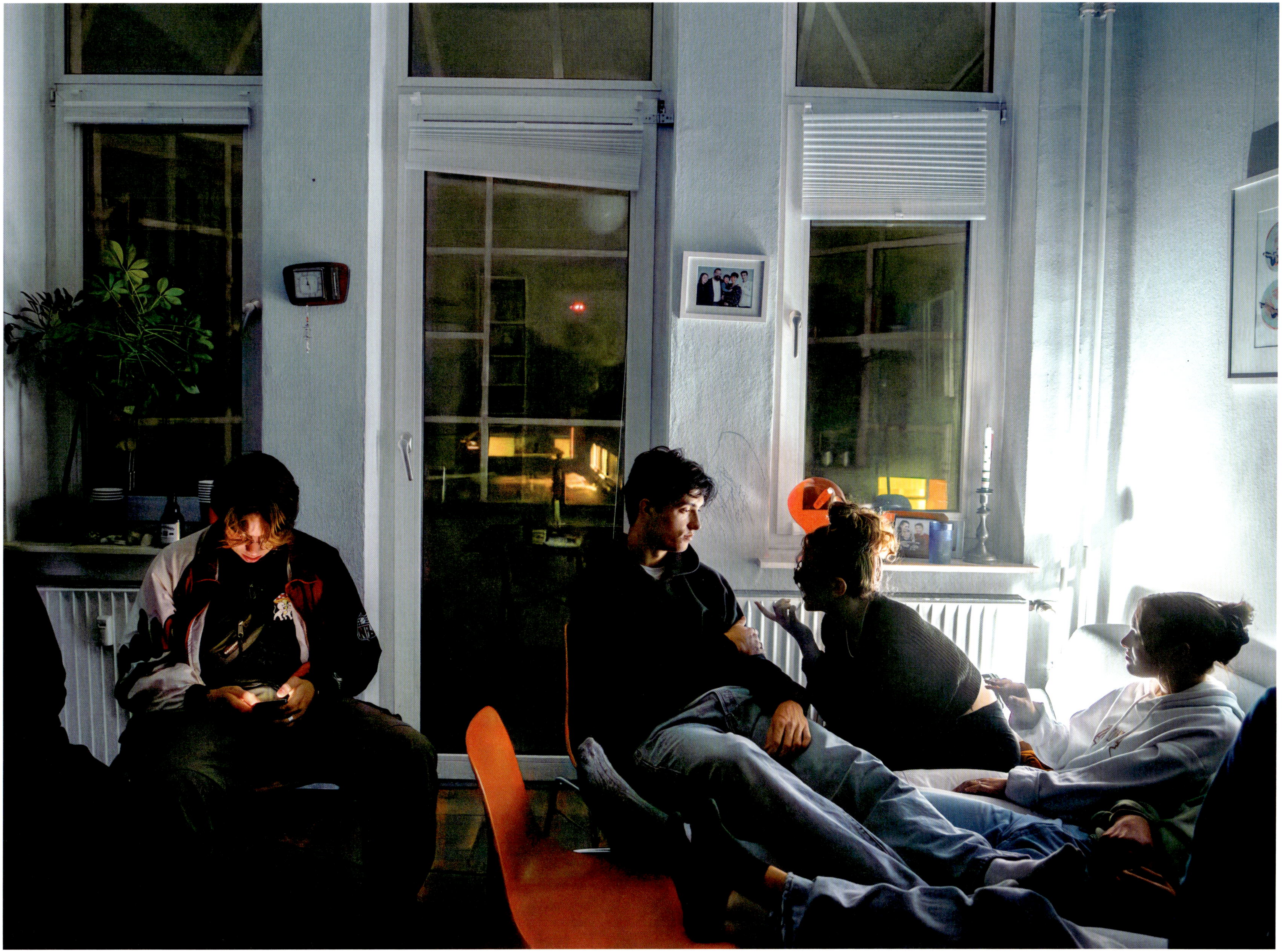

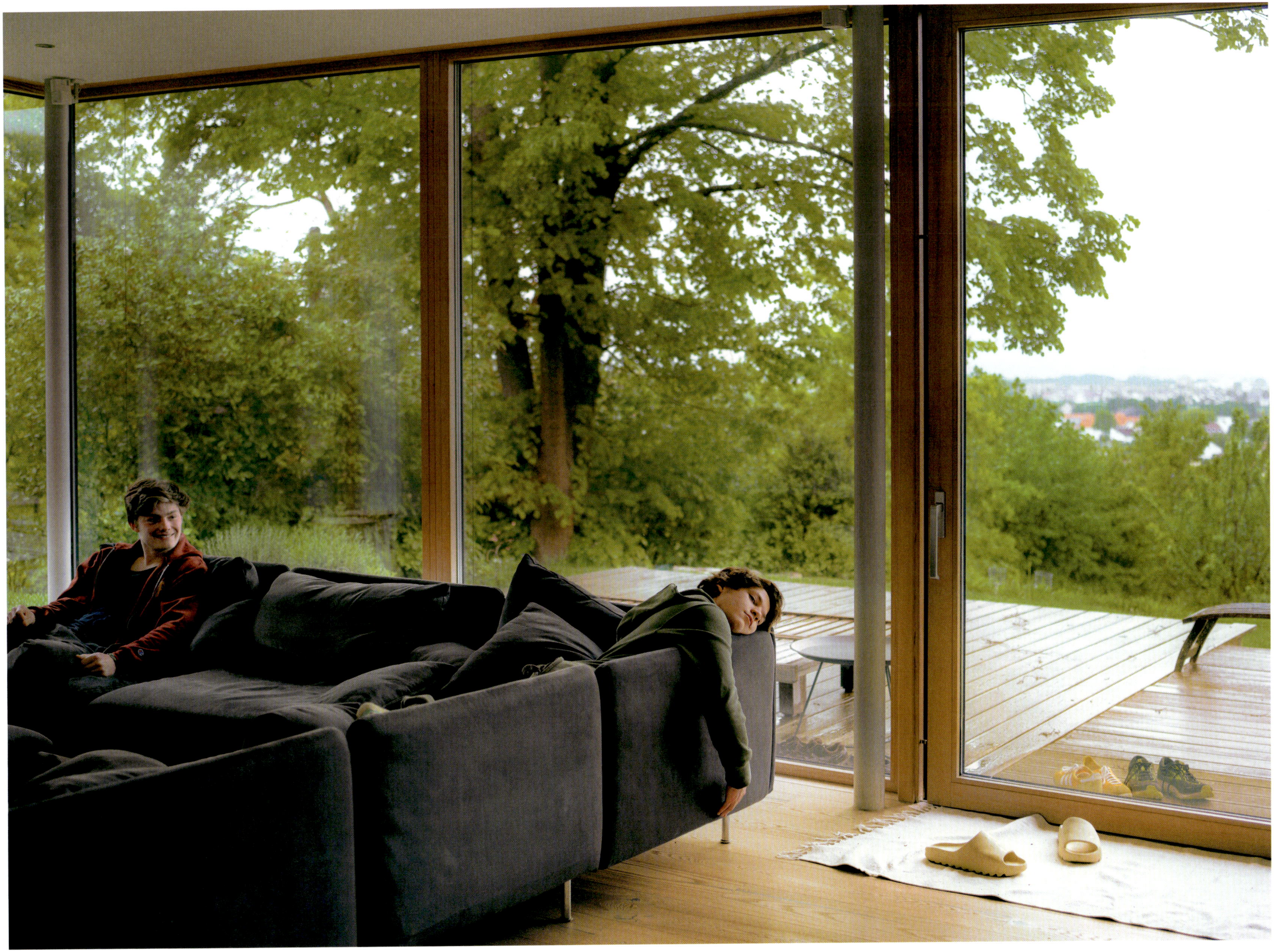

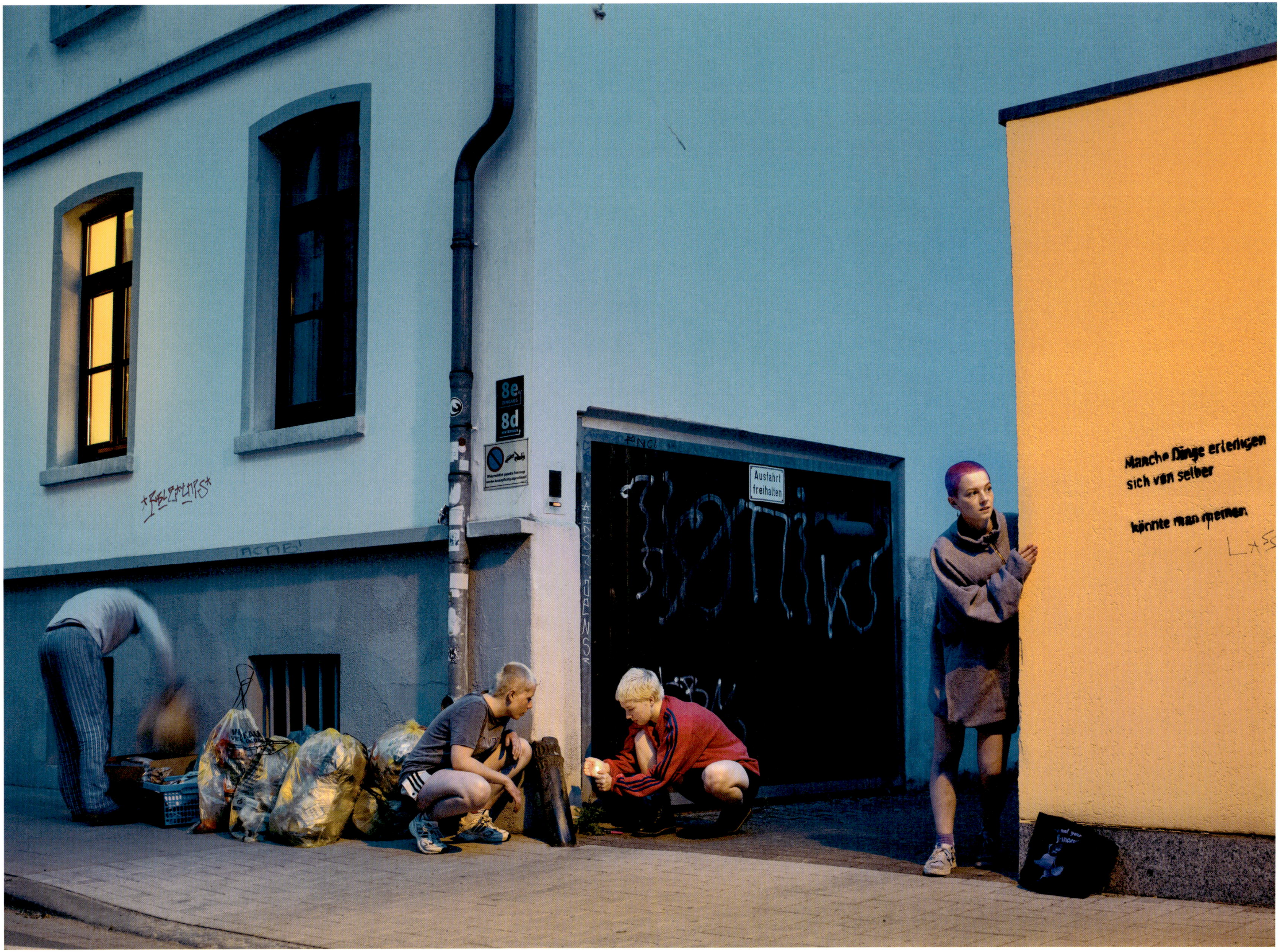
8e
8d
Ausfahrt
freihalten
Manche Dinge erledigen
sich von selber
könnte man meinen

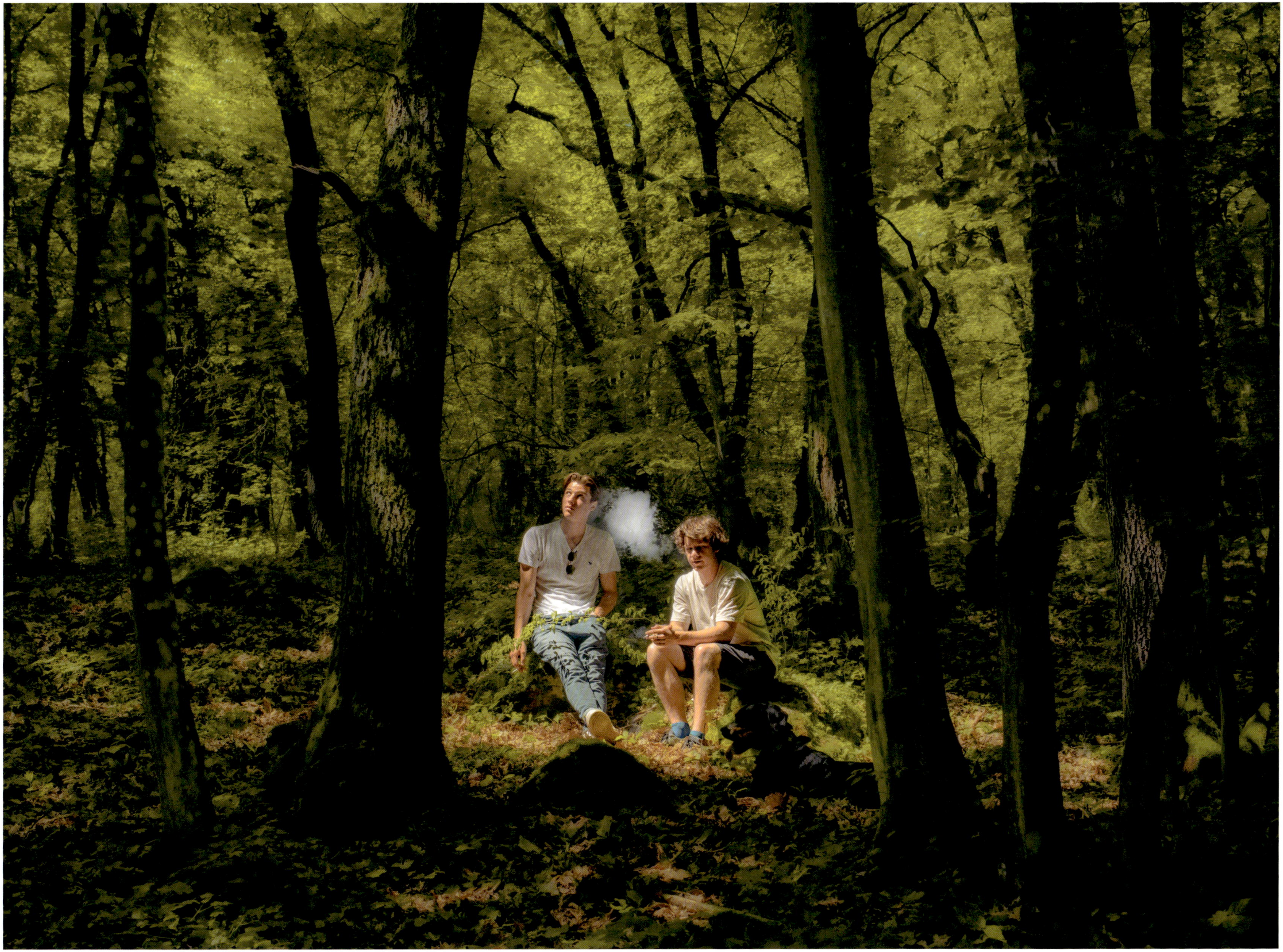

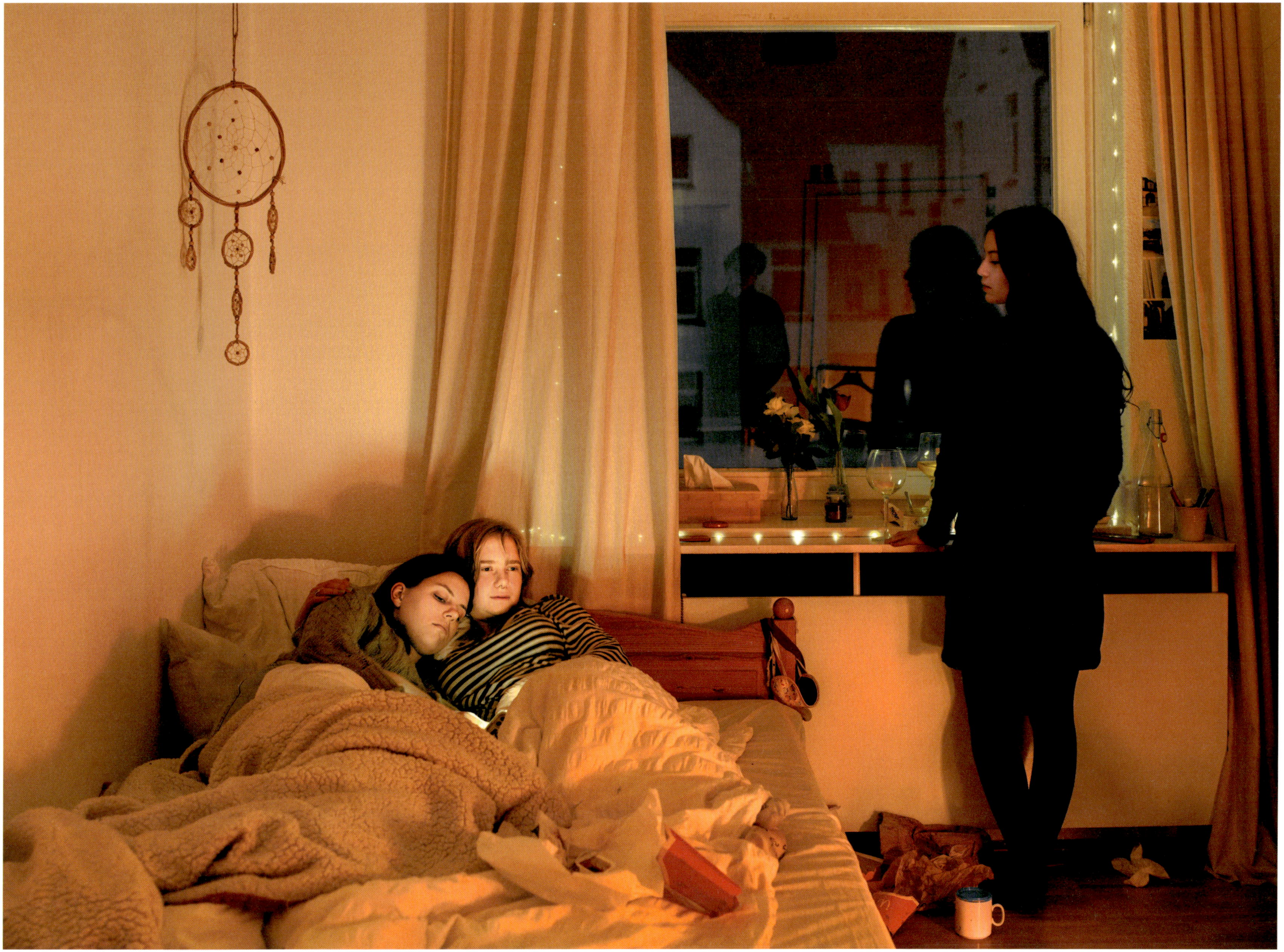

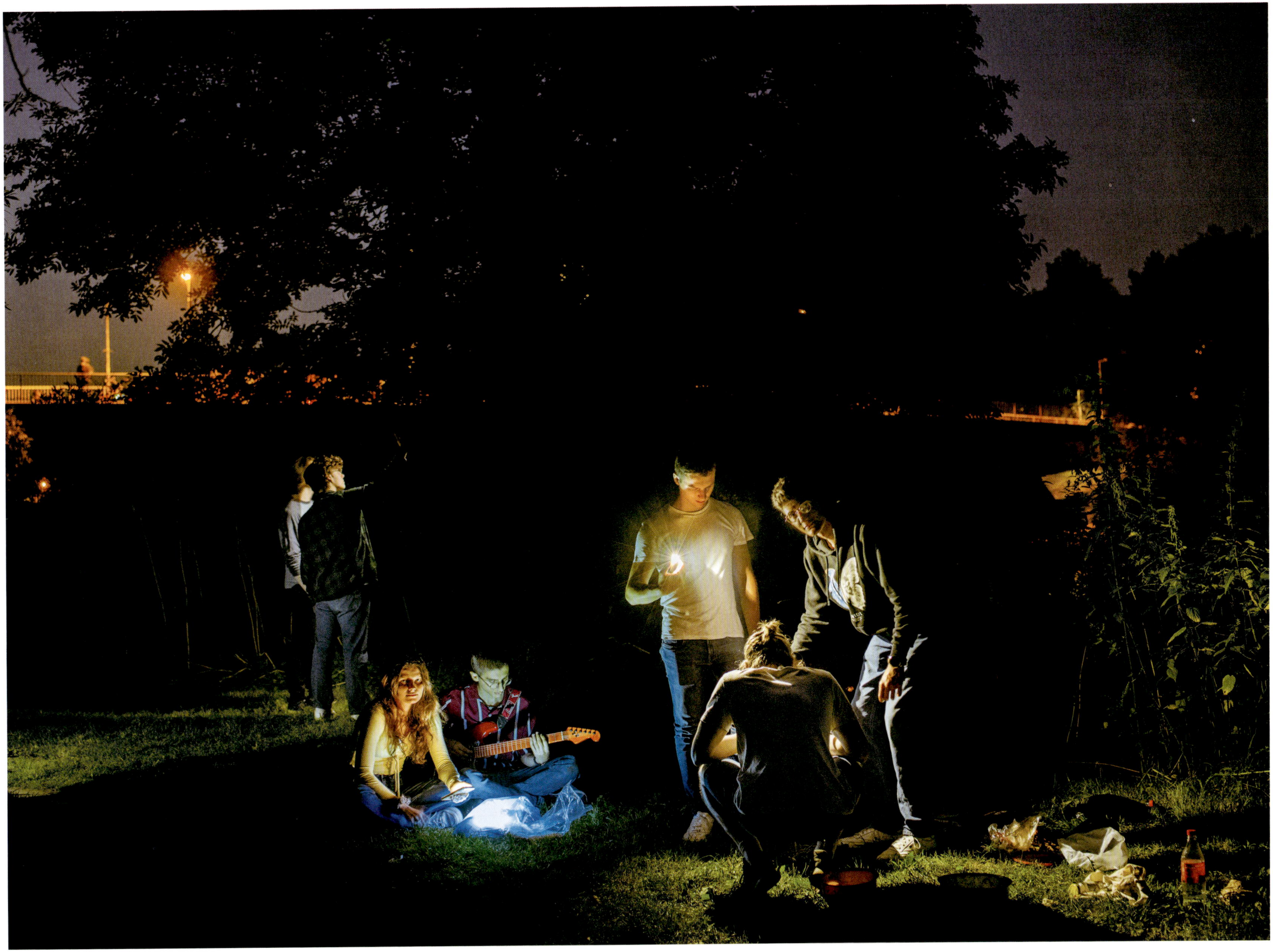

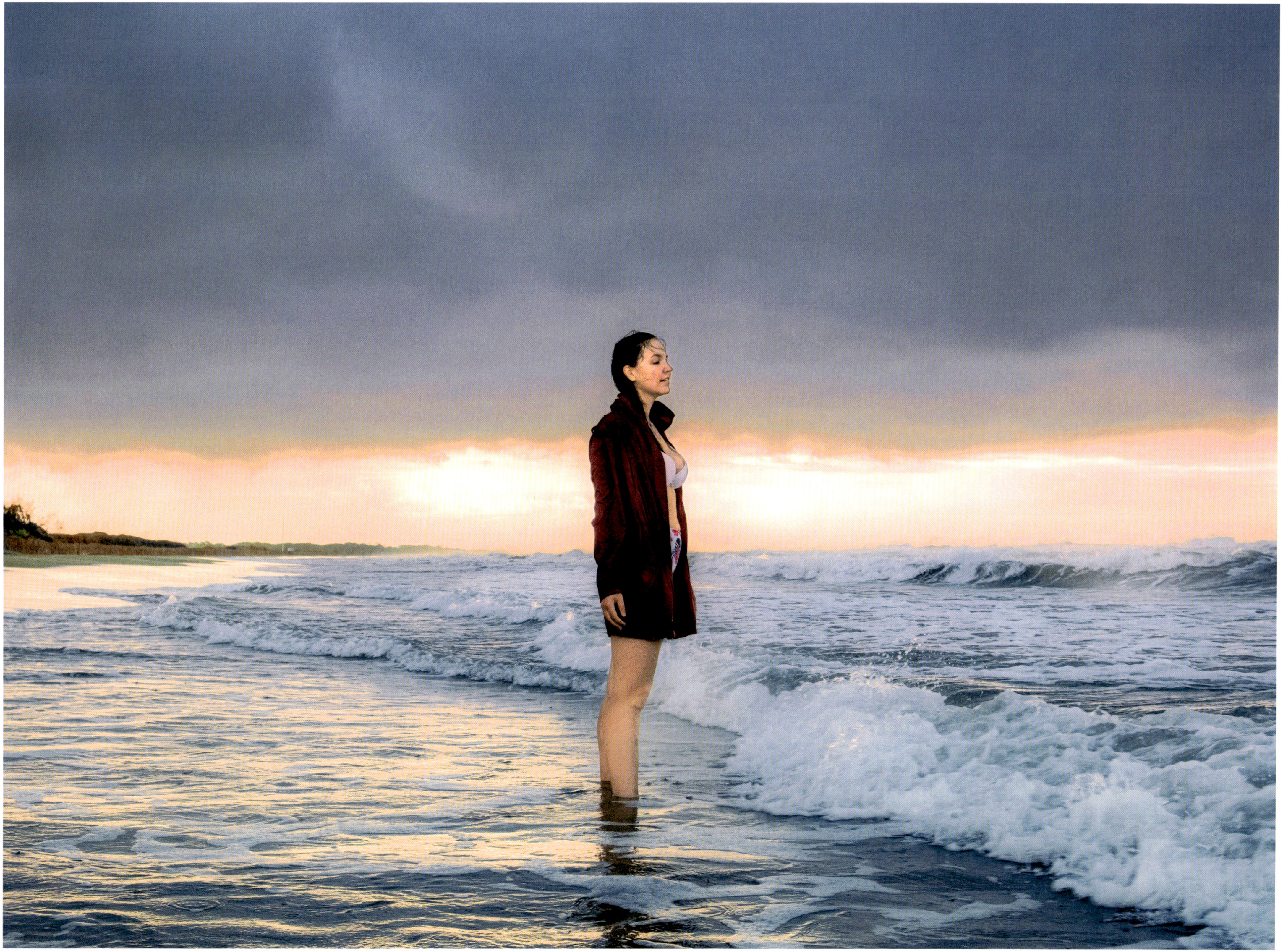

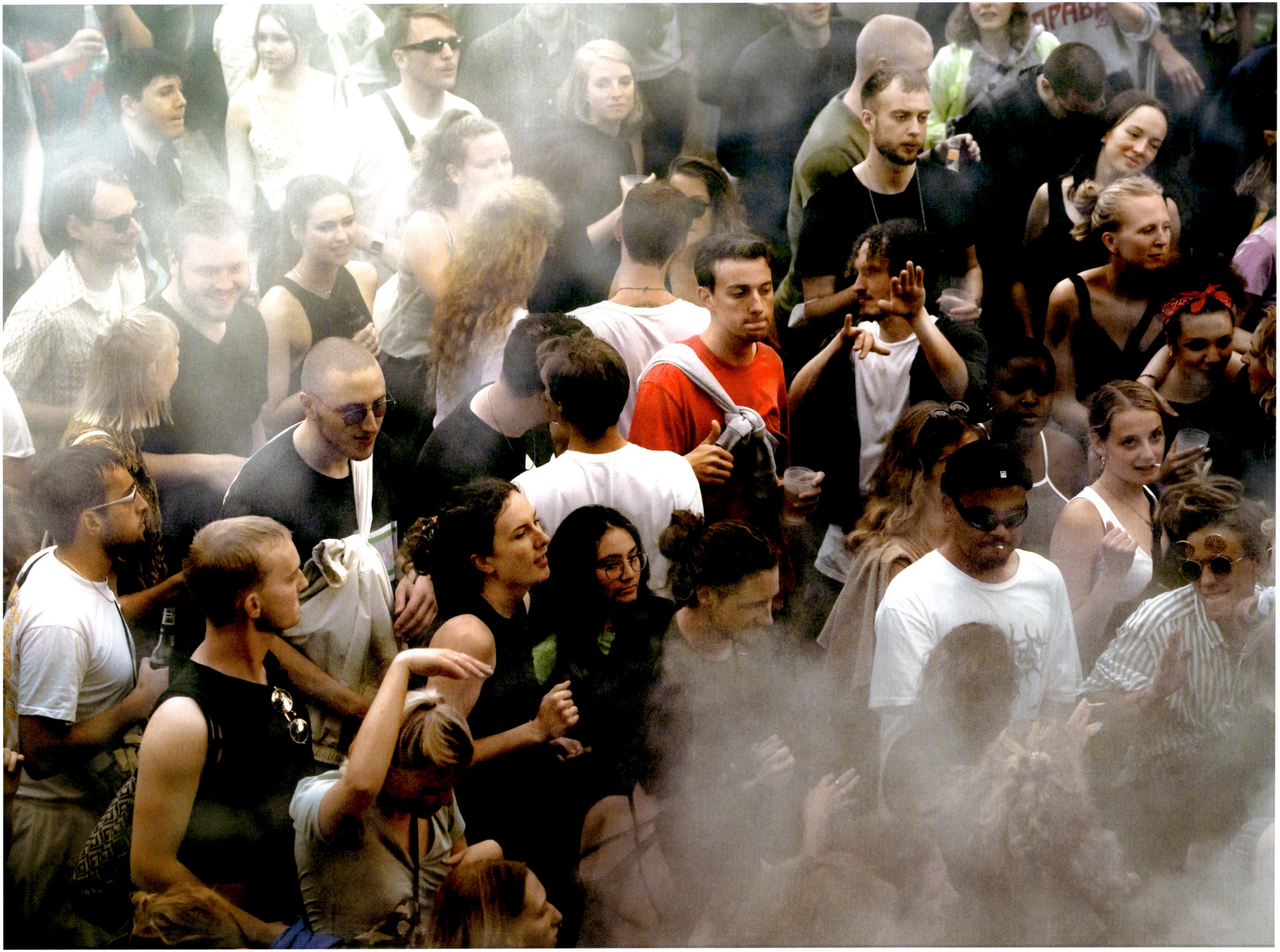

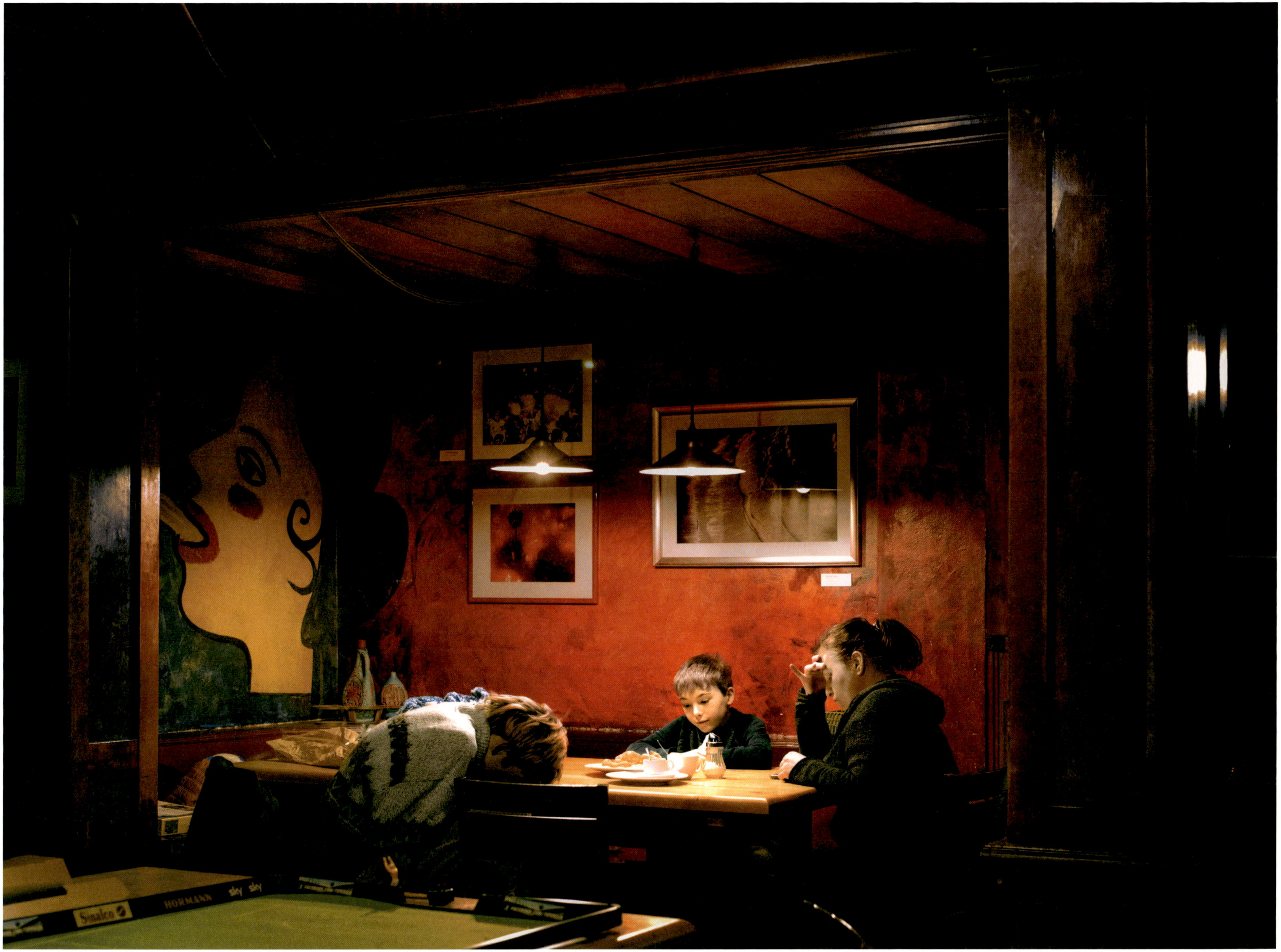
Sinalco
HORMANN
sky sky

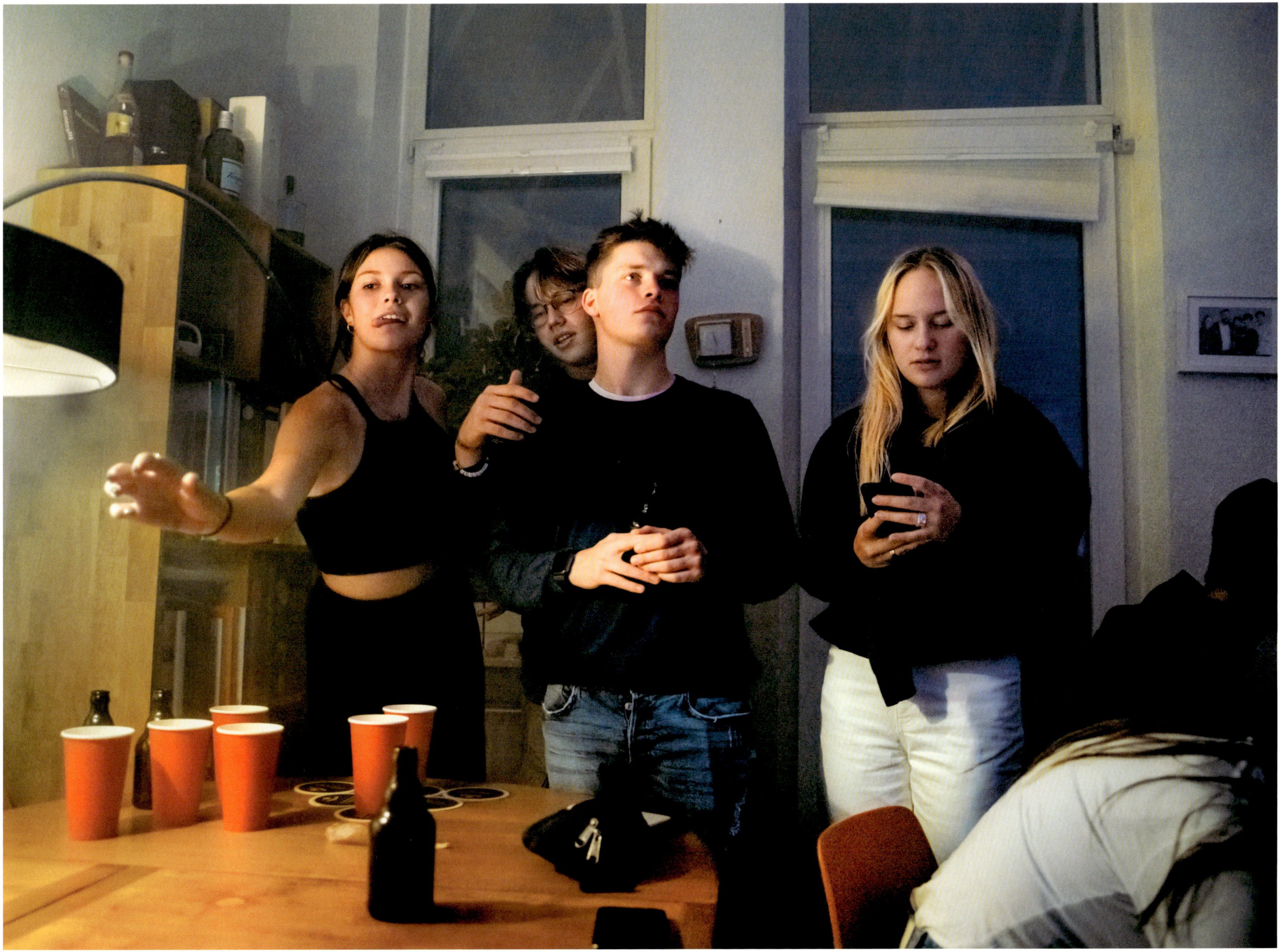

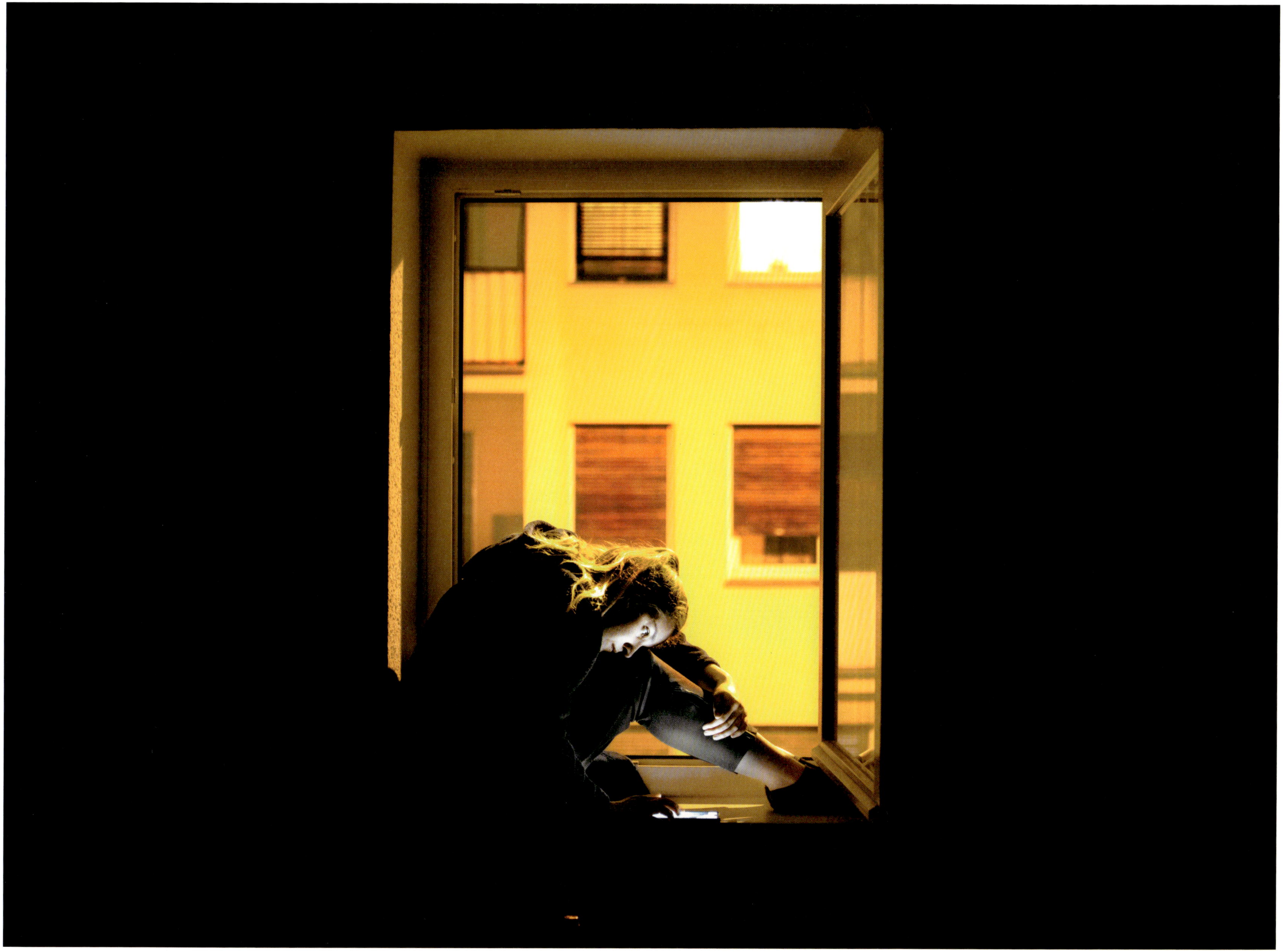

I was visiting my parents when the news first spoke of a lockdown. Thrilled at the thought of what I saw as an extended vacation, I wrote a note on the kitchen table: 'Unis are closed, might stay a few more days.' I was so full of energy that I did not finish the sentence, the note ended at, 'might stay a fe-.' The joy did not last long. At some point, I had exhausted the Netflix watchlist and done all the lazy things I would normally feel guilty for and then I wished I could go back to university. When the online lectures started, I realised quickly that I couldn't cope with this form of study at all. I needed my usual walk to the university, and to share annoyed glances as the classes dragged on. Covid pulled the rug from under my feet and revealed there was no solid ground beneath it. It took some time to realise I was not alone. Many of the people I photographed were the friends I had been missing for months. It was not difficult to explain to them what pictures I was looking for—we were all in the middle of it and knew how the other was feeling. The camera was my personal tool in processing the weight of our disorientation. Between observation, staging and the recreation of memories, I tried to find ways to express the diffuse of feelings of growing up in the 'time of corona.'

Not knowing where to hold on when everything is shaking around you may just be natural during the period in life when one is no longer a child, but not yet an adult. The pandemic worked as a catalyst to my disorientation, bringing to light the inner conflicts that had been well contained by the right environment and sufficient distraction. They finally broke free and took the space they had always silently demanded.

Before the pandemic, one in ten German teenagers showed symptoms of depression. At the end of the first lockdown, it was one in four. Many of my friends had trouble reconnecting with their social lives after the lockdown and I was no different. I have yet to go back to university.

The message I wrote to my parents at the beginning of the pandemic was preserved in a picture frame as a document of time. For months, it sat in a moving box in my new flat share. It took some time until I could unpack.

—Valentin Goppel

In German the last days of December are described as a time between the years. The old is over and the new has not yet begun. In a state of limbo one lies around both paralysed and hopeful.

Thank you to all the people who decided to be part of this project and its pictures. Together with you I did not feel alone, I can only hope that you felt the same way.

Thank you Stuart Smith and the fantastic team at GOST for the intense and beautiful collaboration in the making of this book.

Thank you Lara Huck and Amélie Schneider for your trust in this project from the beginning.

Thank you Andrea Diefenbach and Dr. Karen Fromm for the both personal and productive guidance during the making of the project.

Thank you Florian Hammerich. The word 'mentor' is hardly loaded enough to describe your all-inclusive support.

Thank you to my love Mia, for putting up with my work and worries.

Also, thank you to many other people without whom this work wouldn't exist in the form it is now: Josephine Altmeyer, Hana Bejlková, Benton Böhm, Nicole Büsing and Heiko Klaas, Paris Chong, Hubert Denk, Nick Drake, Ann-Sophie Ellinghausen, Melena Elsner, Ophelia Feltz, Daniela Goldmann, Paul Hartinger, Michael Hartmann, Karin Kaufmann and the LOBA-Team, Stork Kiosk, Johanna Langenhoff, Sarah Meier, Eduardo Navarro, Ludwig Nikulski, Gabriel Prödl, Jan Wille, Simón Wlasiczuck, Lena Wöhler, Raimund Zaikowski

Finally, thank you to my parents.

Zwischen den Jahren
First published in 2023
by GOST Books, London

info@gostbooks.com
gostbooks.com

Edited and designed by GOST:
Rossella Castello, Katie Clifford,
Gemma Gerhard, Justine Hucker,
Allon Kaye, Eleanor Macnair,
Claudia Paladini, Ana Rocha

Printed in Italy by EBS

British Library cataloguing-in-publication data. A catalogue record of this book is available from the British Library.

Isbn 978-1-915423-17-7